The Adoption of Black Children

The Adoption of Black Children

Counteracting Institutional Discrimination

Dawn Day
Response Analysis Corporation

Lexington Books
D.C. Heath and Company
Lexington, Massachusetts
Toronto

Library of Congress Cataloging in Publication Data

Day, Dawn.
    The adoption of Black children.

    Includes bibliographical references and index.
    1. Adoption—United States. 2. Afro-American children—United
States. 3. Interracial adoption—United States. I. Title.
HV875.D36   362.7'34   77-18585
ISBN 0-669-02107-5

Published simultaneously in Canada.

Printed in the United States of America.

International Standard Book Number: 0-669-02107-5

Library of Congress Catalog Card Number: 77-18585

Contents

List of Tables

Preface

As family and friends gathered around the bassinet, someone admiringly commented: "So young and already the daughter of a general!"

Some are born to privilege; others are not. This book is about a group of children who have no family at all, until they are adopted. It is also a book about racial discrimination—discrimination which occurs in a variety of ways:

There is the discrimination which occurs when all an agency's resources are put into placing white children (chapter 2).

There is the discrimination which occurs when black mothers are not permitted to give up their babies for adoption and white women are (chapter 1).

There is the discrimination which occurs when no one takes the legal steps necessary to free for adoption a black child abandoned in a foster home (chapter 1).

There is the discrimination which occurs when qualified black people apply but are not permitted to adopt (chapters 2 and 3).

There is the discrimination which occurs when a black child is denied a permanent home because the only available adopters are white and the agency does not place black children with white adopters (chapter 6).

There is the discrimination which occurs when relatives refuse to accept an adopted child, just because the child is black and has been adopted by whites (chapter 6).

This book is also a study of adoption as a system. For only by understanding the pressures on social agencies and adoption workers can one hope to change those pressures and improve the adoption opportunities of black children (chapters 4 and 5).

The book is sprinkled with suggestions on how agencies can increase their placements with black adopters. The final chapter shows how doing all the right things completely changed the adoption situation in one city, Detroit.

An unfinished thread for me is the role of organized religion. To the extent that agencies with religious sponsorship restrict placements to their own sect's members, many good potential adopters among blacks are excluded. This is so because many blacks are not members of the mainstream religious groups which sponsor social agencies. Learning the extent of such exclusionary practices and the social forces which bring them into being would be an important step toward reform.

Acknowledgments

It is close to ten years since I first took up my interest in the adoption of black children. As with any work that long in the making, this book has benefited from the help, cooperation, advice, and encouragement of a number of people and organizations. (Their participation in these various ways, of course, does not mean that they endorse my conclusions.)

I am particularly grateful to the supervisors and staff members at the twenty-four Washington, D.C., and Baltimore adoption agencies who participated in the survey reported in chapter 2. The participating agencies were the Alexandria Department of Public Welfare, Anne Arundel County Department of Social Services, Arlington Department of Human Resources, Associated Catholic Charities of Baltimore, Baltimore City Department of Social Services, Baltimore County Department of Social Services, Barker Foundation, Board of Child Care of the Methodist Church, Catholic Charities of the District of Columbia, Catholic Families and Children's Services of Northern Virginia, Children's Home Society, Church Mission of Help, the District of Columbia Department of Social Services, Fairfax County Department of Social Services, Family and Child Services of the District of Columbia, Family and Children's Society of Baltimore, Jewish Family and Children's Services of Baltimore, Jewish Social Service Agency of Washington, D.C., Lutheran Social Services, Maryland Children's Aid, Montgomery County Department of Social Services, Peirce Warwick, Prince Georges County Department of Social Services, and the St. Sophia Greek Orthodox Adoption Service.

Without the consent of Patricia M. Pettiford, director of the Office of Research and Evaluation of the New York City Department of Social Services, the study reported in chapter 3 could not have been completed. The help of all the staff members at the Division of Adoption Services, where the study was carried out, is also much appreciated.

Others helped in a variety of ways. Some people read drafts of chapters; others gave information and materials. Some shared their thoughts; others disagreed mightily. They were Hanna Adams, Elizabeth Alexander, Claire Berman, Elizabeth Berry, Peggy Brown, Barbara Chappell, Dan Claster, Marjorie Dandrich, Kay Donley, Ms. DuMez, Michael Flynn, Peter Forsythe, Claire Gaines, Ursula Gallagher, Pat Gambino, Phyllis Gold, Hanna Grossman, Clayten Hagen, Al Herbert, Aeolian Jackson, Carl Kessler, Paul Kuczkowski, Rael Isaacs, Ed Laumann, John Leonard, Ann Maney, Henry Meyer, Marilyn Monk, Paul Montagna, Leora Neal, Julie Oktay, Charles Olds, Malinda Berry Orlin, Susan Page, Ann Peabody, Jerry Peabody, Rosemary Sarri, Jeannine Sawers, Elaine Schwartz, Nadine Shaberman, Ann Shyne, Francis Snider, Stuart Stimmel, Beverly Stubee, Cecelia Sudia, Elizabeth Taylor, Howard Wachtel, Laine Waggoner, Linda Walker, and Carol Williams.

Judy Fliegenspan shared with me the initial dream of writing this book and helped write the first outline. Her other commitments prevented her from continuing as coauthor, but chapter 3 remains hers.

Sydney Duncan, the director of Homes for Black Children in Detroit, was very generous with her time and thoughts as I wrote chapter 7.

Nathan Schmukler, dean of the School of Social Science of Brooklyn College, provided much-appreciated funds to cover the cost of typing.

Finishing the final draft was made much less painful by the careful proofing of Nancy Ginsburg and by the extraordinary competence and patience of the typist, Ann Peterman.

The actual writing of the chapters was carried out in the past few months. During this period my husband, Reuben Cohen, helped me greatly by providing his own special kind of support and encouragement and by tolerating my single-minded commitment to finishing this book.

Trends in "Adoptable" Children

Alan, 3 years old, is a handsome, medium-complexioned black toddler who is learning to talk. Alan receives medication for convulsions and bronchial asthma. His health problems are well controlled by proper medication monitoring. He is an active and affectionate child.

Anita is a 9-year-old black girl. She is attractive and warm and likes to sing in the church choir. She is in the third grade and considered to be educably mentally retarded.

Alvon and Dominique are two black brothers who must be placed together. Alvon is 9 years old and in good health. He is active and strong-willed, and does average work in school, although he has the potential to do superior work. He is presently in therapy for minor behavioral problems. Alvon loves the outdoors, running and playing football. He is very protective of his 6-year-old brother, Dominique, who is also in good health and very active. It took a while for Dominique to settle down in school, but he is doing fine now. He is rather strong-willed and will test his new parents. Like Alvon, he enjoys physical activities and the outdoors.

Shawn is a very attractive 4-year-old black boy with a medium-brown complexion and dark brown hair and eyes. He has no known allergies or medical problems. He is active, talkative, and really charming. He likes to play and go on outings.

Renee is a 6-year-old black girl with average intelligence. She loves attention and is friendly and inquisitive.

Glenda is a warm, friendly 9-year-old black girl who is an average student in the fourth grade. She is outgoing and generally healthy, although she does have a tendency toward bronchitis.

Jonathan is a 10-year-old black boy who is making normal progress in school. He is used to a rural setting and has been in Cub Scouts. He likes sports; he is pleasant, sensitive, and talkative.[1]

These short paragraphs are typical descriptions that adoption agencies give out to other agencies and adoptive parent groups as homes are sought for children available for adoption. The children described always have had four parents, and the unlucky ones have had six parents, eight parents, or even more. The first parents, of course, are the biological parents, and after them come foster parents. If no foster parents are found, the youngster ends up in an institution.

How many black children are there in the United States who need adoptive homes? The incredible answer is that no one knows for sure. Hundreds of adoption agencies around the country have legal custody of thousands of black youngsters, but the agencies have no single organization to which they must report the children for whom they have been unable to find permanent homes.

There are estimates, of course, and these range from a conservative 40,000 to 80,000 and higher.[2] The *Opportunity* surveys in 1973 and 1974, national surveys involving several hundred agencies, revealed that black children accounted for about 20 percent of all children placed but 40 percent of the combined backlog of all children awaiting adoption.[3]

People in the adoption field usually distinguish between the 1960s when there was an abundance of children available for adoption and the 1970s when, because of the increased availability of abortion, many fewer children have been available for adoption. The change has been most dramatic with respect to white babies; however, black babies, too, are in somewhat scarcer supply. In addition, a larger number of young mothers are keeping their babies, but this change has been more gradual.[4] Even with the increase in abortions, black children are still in abundant supply. In 1969, shortly before the changes in the legal status of abortion, a survey of 240 adoption agencies revealed there were only 39 nonwhite homes approved for every 100 nonwhite children reported as needing adoptive placement. In 1975, a smaller survey of 57 agencies showed an improvement. Then there were 85 black homes approved for every 100 black children reported as needing adoptive placement. Thus in 1975, a total of 57 agencies accepted for adoption 533 black children for whom they did not find adoptive homes.[5]

The need for black adoptive homes does not end with the uncounted number of black children legally free for adoption. As long as there is a backlog of black children awaiting adoption, there will be other black children living in foster homes and institutions who also need permanent homes but whom the agencies and courts do not bother to free for adoption because no homes are available. Similarly, some black parents who feel they are unable to care for a child nonetheless will not give up the child, fearing correctly that their child may never be adopted. Or the parents may try desperately to relinquish but be unable to find an agency willing to take the child.

Trying to Give Up a Child for Adoption

In the late 1800s, an adoption agency in the District of Columbia kept a big basket on the doorstep. The yard was landscaped so that a mother could place her baby in the basket, ring the doorbell, and then run behind a high shrub and watch to make sure her baby was picked up.[6]

Such an arrangement would have been helpful to reluctant mothers in the

1960s as well. Evidence that black women and some white women could not
get help at adoption agencies during the 1960s comes from a 1966 study done
in the District of Columbia. For a full year, fifteen social agencies in the District
of Columbia (including eight adoption agencies) kept a record of every woman
who approached them seeking advice with respect to her unborn child and
whether the woman succeeded in having at least one interview with a social
worker. At adoption agencies, almost half of all the requests for help from
white women resulted in at least one interview; less than a quarter of the requests from black women had this happy outcome (table 1-1).

From the point of view of someone interested in whether women are being
given the opportunity to relinquish a child for adoption if they so desire, the
1966 study stops too soon. A woman could well be "accepted" in the terms of
this study—that is, seen for one interview—but still discover, after childbirth,
that the agency would not accept relinquishment of her child.

Despite its shortcomings, the 1966 study is a very useful one. It illustrates
some of the factors influencing social workers in their acceptance or rejection
of particular mothers seeking service.

The most privileged woman from the point of view of acceptance rates,
was the single white woman under 16 who was living in the District of Columbia
and was one to three months pregnant. The most disadvantaged was the married
black woman, aged 30 or older, who lived outside the District of Columbia

Table 1-1
**Percentage of Women Seeking Adoption Counseling Granted at Least One
Interview, by Type of Agency and by Race of Mother, Washington, D.C., 1966**

	White	Black	Black and Other	Total
All mothers[a]	54	38	39	48
All applications[b]	47	32	33	42
Adoption agencies	45	24	26	38
Maternity homes	49	38	39	45
Other agencies	55	81	77	72

Source: District of Columbia Department of Public Welfare, Committee on Regulations,
Unmarried Mother Registration Project Report, April 1967, tables 4, 8A, and 8B.

[a]Each woman is counted only once regardless of the number of applications she made.
Mothers applying to public welfare only for financial assistance (Aid to Families with Dependent Children) were not included in the study.

[b]Each application is counted separately.

metropolitan area and was one to three months pregnant with an in-wedlock child (table 1-2).

It is of interest that the characteristics which handicapped the white mother hurt the black mother even more. For example, for both whites and blacks, the acceptance rate was highest for young mothers under 16 and lowest for older

Table 1-2

Percentage of Women Seeking Adoption Counseling Granted at Least One Interview,[a] by Race and Other Characteristics of the Mother, Washington, D.C., 1966

	Black and Other	White
Age		
15 and under	54	60
16 to 17	47	58
18 to 19	37	58
20 to 29	35	57
30 and over	24	48
Marital status		
Single	40	56
Married, child out of wedlock	34	32
Married, child in wedlock	13	28
Residence		
D.C.	42	57
Metropolitan area surrounding D.C.	35	56
Outside D.C. metropolitan area	29	51
Number of months before expected date of delivery		
Baby already born	41	49
Less than 3 months	34	45
3 to 5.9 months	45	60
6 months or more	39	61
Total	39	54

Source: District of Columbia Department of Public Welfare, Committee on Regulations, *Unmarried Mother Registration Project Report,* April 1967, table E.

[a]The acceptance rates by age, marital status, and so on are for nonwhites (not blacks), all social agencies (not adoption agencies), and all applications (not all women requesting help) because the more specific data are not available. The 15 social agencies include 8 adoption agencies, 4 maternity homes, Travelers' Aid, the Salvation Army, and the Red Cross.

The nonoccurrence of an interview is a somewhat ambiguous category. The interview may not have occurred either because the agency refused to make an appointment or because the woman canceled. The fact that one-fourth of the women applied to more than one agency strongly suggests that agency rejection was common. There is little reason to expect that the proportion of women canceling appointments voluntarily should vary by race.

women. In every age group, however, the acceptance rate for whites was higher than that for blacks. To put it another way, the young teenage black mother was less likely to get service at an agency than a white mother of 22.

Acceptance rates for both whites and blacks were highest for residents of the District of Columbia and lowest for mothers who originally lived outside the area. Mothers currently living outside their home residence area are probably most in need of assistance from social agencies. They are the women who could not face living at home while they bore an unplanned child. They are also the women whose families could not face having a pregnant daughter living at home.

Place of residence was a much more important factor with regard to acceptance of black than of white mothers. White mothers in the least favored category—residence outside the District of Columbia metropolitan area—had higher acceptance rates than black mothers in the most favored category—residence in the District of Columbia.

Overall, the 1966 data present a striking picture of inequality of opportunity. In disproportionate numbers, black mothers were turned away from adoption agencies.

The main institutional innovation brought into the Washington, D.C., scene following the 1966 study was the Information and Referral Service for Unmarried Parents. The purpose of the service was to eliminate the need for women to make repeated attempts to be accepted at adoption agencies. The part-time social worker at the referral service would keep calling until she located a willing agency. In all, the service had contact with 611 women in the first two years of operation, ending in October 1969.

The referral service was instrumental in securing social agency service for black mothers, although perhaps not in the way anticipated at the time the service was established.

If race had not been a factor in acceptance for social agency service, one would expect to find the proportion of black mothers on adoption agency caseloads to be pretty much the same. Instead, in 1970 the proportion of black mothers on caseloads in the seven private District of Columbia adoption agencies varied from 0 to 43 percent. Ninety-eight percent of the mothers being helped by the public agency were black.

What accounted for this wide variation? The answer lies in the policies of the adoption agencies and the referral service itself. The referral service sent women to the public agency only as a last resort.[7] Apparently there was always some agency willing to take another white mother. This meant that virtually no white women were referred to the public agency. On the other hand, the private agencies set limits on the number of black mothers they would accept. Two agencies would not see black mothers at all. The two private agencies most active in helping blacks had explicit mechanisms which limited the number of black women on their caseloads. One agency did this through a requirement of religious affiliation—the mother or father had to have been baptized in the sponsoring church. At the other agency, black mothers were accepted until the agency foster homes for black children were full. In 1970 the agency had fifteen such foster homes. Thus, as a result of a variety of policies and practices, the vast majority of black mothers seeking adoption help ended up at the public agency.

Advice from Social Workers

The lack of homes for black children was reflected in the counseling given to mothers at the agencies. In 1970, supervisors in eighteen Washington and Baltimore agencies were asked the question, "In counseling a black natural mother, do you mention the agency may have difficulty in placing the child?" Fourteen answered in the affirmative. Their comments illustrate their thinking:

> Yes. We try to be honest and reassuring. [We] commit ourselves to finding the best home possible.

> Yes. We are needing to say we may not readily find a home.

> Yes. We are very frank with her. We have never had a baby go without a home, though it takes longer.

> Yes. Black mothers are told placement might not be a possibility, and sometimes they say they want the child back if it isn't adopted.

When asked whether they felt mentioning the difficulty affected the decision the mother made concerning relinquishment, supervisors commented in a variety of ways:

> I hope we don't initiate it; but if she asks, I would say it is somewhat more difficult than for a white baby, but we would find a home. There isn't any stated policy on this. I'm sure it would [affect the woman's decision], though it depends on the way it is mentioned. Most of the workers would put it in a positive light.

> We say we will accept the baby if they want, but that there may be some wait before permanent placement. We don't let this become a factor in the woman's decision.

> Oh, yes, of course. I don't think any agency would deny that [it affects the woman's decision].

Some supervisors felt that the black mothers knew about the difficulty of finding homes even before they came to the agencies.

Yes. Yes, we are perfectly honest. The baby may be older. The girls know anyway. This affects some girls keeping their babies. We tell them we arrange the best foster care possible.

Yes. I think women know before they come in. We mention difficulty in placing to black women just as we do to women who are mothers of children who are hard to place for other reasons.

The girls all bring this up. Just recently there was an article in the newspaper saying unplaced babies are 4 to 6 years old. This led to a whole rash of calls from girls who had relinquished babies to the agency earlier.

The responses of the four agency supervisors who reported that their agencies do not mention the difficulty of placement to black mothers are also of interest.

No. We have stopped mentioning that since we have the program of long-term foster care [begun three years earlier].

I doubt it because through [another agency] we haven't had any problems.

No, not any more. We used to say we don't know how long it will take, but now we don't. In (Virginia) we now have a shortage of black babies. [Supervisors at the other four Virginia agencies participating in this study did not share her view.]

Prior to 1968 this was done. Since November 1968, the [unmarried parent service] has accepted all women who have applied. They take relinquishment when she is ready. She does not have to wait. She can call back to see if placement is done. The discouraging of women may still occur at intake which is done outside this section.

It is noteworthy that two of the four agency supervisors who reported that their social workers did not tell black women that placement might be difficult did so because they transferred the children to another agency or placed them in long-term foster care. In fact, in Washington, D.C., and Baltimore in late 1970, the number of black children needing homes had reached crisis proportions. There were more children awaiting adoption than had been placed in the entire previous year (table 1-3).

The purpose here is to compare the differential opportunities of black and white mothers. We do not mean to imply that black mothers should have been told their children would be placed quickly in adoptive homes when this was not the case. Rather, the need was for the agencies to find more adoptive homes for black children and hence to create a situation where the black mother could

Table 1-3
Children Needing Homes Compared with Children Adopted, by Race,
Washington, D.C., and Baltimore, 1969-1970

| | Number[a] (Percent) | | |
	Black[b]	White and Other	Total
Children needing homes[c]	333 (71)	138 (29)	471 (100)
Children adopted[d]	259 (14)	1580 (86)	1839 (100)
Children needing homes per 100 children adopted the previous year	129	9	4

Source: District of Columbia and Baltimore Adoption Agency Survey.

[a]The table includes data from the 21 adoption agencies which were asked questions about children awaiting placement. Together these agencies account for 92 percent of the adoptive placements made in 1969 by the 24 agencies in the Washington, D.C., and Baltimore metropolitan areas.

[b]Black placements include placements of all black children, regardless of the race of the adopters.

[c]In late 1970.

[d]For 20 agencies the placement figures are for 1969, and for 1 agency they are for 1970. Most agencies reported their adoption statistics on a calendar-year basis. However, 6 agencies used a fiscal year, and several others used still other 12-month periods such as April to March.

truthfully be told that, if she chose to relinquish, her child would be given a permanent home quickly.

But perhaps the phrase "chose to relinquish" implies too much. Although no systematic data were collected on the issue, in the 1970 interviews in the District of Columbia and Baltimore, several supervisors in private agencies did mention that their agencies did not always accept relinquishment.

> The [main] office tends not to take release until it is sure the baby is adoptable. [Our branch] takes the release anyway, if the problem does not seem too severe. We can find homes for the less-than-perfect baby now.

What happens to the woman whose baby is not adoptable?

> That is my concern, too. We have usually worked with welfare to get them to take the child. It's hard for the girl.

> If the baby is pretty healthy, we say we are confident that we will find a home. We have nine black approved families for babies right now.

What if the child is handicapped, say with a cleft palate? What do you say?

> We are worried about the prematurity bit. We said to a woman [recent-
> ly], "our doctor does not feel we can place this baby for adoption. You
> should talk to the [welfare department] about long-term care." The
> girl was very resentful. I tell the social workers to mention this during
> counseling. There is no point in filling up the foster homes with babies
> we cannot place.
>
> [We mention the difficulty of finding an adoptive home] from the point
> of intake, but stand ready to accept the child or to work through the
> [local] department of social services.

One would expect that the failure or inability of agencies to provide adoption services for black mothers would have a cumulative effect. As negative
stories would circulate in a community, proportionately fewer and fewer
black mothers would even think to apply for help. Alternatively, if something
happened to make black women feel that an agency might help them, even
more would apply. In fact, this was the case. Several agency officials reported
that as their agencies had begun to advertise for black adopters, the agencies had
also experienced an increase in inquiries from black mothers.

Thus the agencies reduced the oversupply of black babies in a number of
ways: refusing counseling to expectant mothers; telling mothers that their
babies may not be adopted for a long time, if ever; or refusing to accept relinquishment. Some agencies used special rules to eliminate some women. For
example, one or more of the District of Columbia and Baltimore agencies
refused to provide service unless the expectant father was involved in counseling
also and signed relinquishment papers, the mother contacted the agency before
the baby was born, the mother paid a fee, the agency had foster homes for black
children, the mother or father was of the same religion as the organization
sponsoring the agency, and the mother was a resident of the community.

Was the situation in Washington, D.C., and Baltimore in the late 1960s
similar to that in other large metropolitan areas across the United States? The
research and observations of Bernstein, Lawder et al., Turitz, Billingsley,
Boothby, Heath, and Fischer show over and over that it was.[8]

More Abortions, Fewer Babies

With the 1970s, a Supreme Court decision, and legislative changes, legal abortion
became a more common alternative to unwanted motherhood.[9] White mothers
came to adoption agencies in fewer and fewer numbers. A "shortage" of white
babies occurred; white couples seeking to adopt found themselves on waiting
lists so long that the child they might one day parent had not been conceived yet.

Newspaper articles were written about a "gray" market in adoption where inter-mediaries were paid high fees to secure white infants for couples impatient to adopt.

In the 1970s black women also turned to abortion in great numbers, as an alternative to undesired motherhood. But the flow of black mothers and babies to adoption agencies did not diminish as soon or as rapidly as the flow of whites. In fact, in the first year or two after abortion became legal, black relinquishments rose. A partial explanation lay in the high cost of private hospital abortions, the common requirement that the abortion be prepaid, and the low-income position of many black women. Public hospitals were usually of little help. Even by 1975, 82 percent of public hospitals still did not permit abortions.[10]

But the availability and cost of abortions were not the whole answer. The practices of adoption agencies across the United States were highly relevant also. In the 1960s and earlier, social agencies had focused almost all their resources on whites. A large portion of the white women who wanted to give a child up for adoption could do so. Thus any switch to abortion led to an almost immediate decline in white relinquishments.

The story for black mothers was different. During the 1960s very few black women who desired adoption had been given that alternative by social agencies. There was a huge unmet need. When abortion became available, many black pregnant women chose it. As with whites, other black mothers still preferred adoption. Now, however, the social agencies were less busy (fewer white mothers were coming in); and, as a result, the agencies were more willing to accept relinquishment of a black child. Between 1969 and 1970 (the first year when abortion was fairly widely available), the number of white children relinquished fell by 7 percent. The number of black children given up for adoption *rose* by 16 percent.[11]

Even after the change in the abortion situation in early 1970, the extent of the shortage of black babies relative to adopters never reached that of white babies. In some places in the mid-1970s supply is just balancing demand. In others, such as Detroit and New York, there is a waiting line of perhaps a year for a healthy, black infant. In still other agencies, there is a surplus of black infants.

What the situation will be in the late 1970s is not clear. The decisions of the Congress, the President, and the Supreme Court, which together prohibit the use of Medicaid funds for abortion, may increase the number of unwanted babies to the point where black babies are again in severe oversupply and mothers of healthy black babies are again being told that there are no adoptive homes.[12]

Faced with a shortage of babies, adoption agencies have changed their practices, making it easier for a woman to get counseling and give up her baby for adoption. A few agencies, whether through religious conviction or personal

self-interest, have slightly increased the supply of babies by withholding information on free and low-cost abortions from the pregnant young women who seek
counseling assistance.[13] [It should be noted that in a number of states a woman
under age cannot get an abortion without the consent of her parents; once the
baby is born, however, a minor can always give up her baby for adoption without her parents' (the grandparents') consent.]

Liberalizing agency policies and extending service to all pregnant women
seeking help could have slowed the decrease in the number of babies coming
into care at a particular agency, but with the change in abortion law, some
decrease was unavoidable. Thus agencies were faced with a challenge to their
existence. Some resolved the issue by going out of business or changing the
focus of their activities. Some continued to do things in the same way but with
a reduced staff. Others began looking around for other sources of children.
They found them in foster care caseloads in this country and in adoption agencies overseas. The definition of an adoptable child changed. Older children,
children with physical or emotional problems, and slow learners began to be
considered adoptable at more agencies.

Obstacles to the Adoption of Foster Children

Even with the reduced supply of infants for adoption, not all agencies turned
in an enthusiastic rush to the foster care caseloads. There were several reasons.
First, foster care was separated bureaucratically within the agencies from adoption activities. The social workers in adoptions might feel they could place a
particular type of child, but the foster care workers would not know, unless a
special effort were made to communicate that fact. And, in fact, unless the
adoption workers make a special effort to find out, they do not know the kinds
of children in foster care.

Second, adopting an older child is something like a marriage. Both the
adopters and the child need to become acquainted with one another's personalities and needs. The skills a social worker needs to help this process along are
different from those needed for placing an infant. Thus the adoption worker
experienced with infants suddenly has a lot to learn if she or he switches to
placing older children. An unknown number have been either unwilling or unable to make that switch.

Then, too, many of the social workers are whites accustomed to working
with white adopters. Many of the foster children are black and need black
adopters. Again, an unknown number of social workers have not been able to
make this adjustment.

In addition, the children in foster care are usually not legally free for
adoption, so several difficult tasks have to be done. One is to decide whether
it is in the child's best interests to continue in foster care until the parent is able

to care for the child again, if ever. If the decision is in favor of adoption, then steps must be taken to free the child legally, either through a voluntary action on the part of the parent or parents or through a court order. In either situation, the parent must be located and talked to, a task which could be quite unpleasant. Finally, the child needs to be prepared for adoption: when foster parents adopt a child who has been living with them for some time, the task can be easy; where the child must be prepared to leave the foster family, the situation can be quite difficult. Also there is the risk that no adoptive parents will ever be found or a potential adopter will be found but somehow the placement will not work out.

Another impediment to finding adoptive homes for foster children is the self-interest of the foster care agency employees. The more children in foster care, the larger the agency's budget and the more jobs for foster care workers and administrators. It is in the government's interest to reduce the number of children in foster care; it is not at all clear that it is in the agency's self-interest to do so.

Finally, there is just the question of time. Foster care agencies—both public and private—already have staff time overfull doing all the tasks associated with foster care. It takes additional resources to examine the foster care caseload and determine which, if any, children should be made eligible for adoption. Where are these resources to come from? And why should the foster care agency put resources into a task as difficult as finding children for adoption when the adoption exhanges are already listing hundreds of older children?

Despite all these problems, a few agencies, whether prodded by reform groups or on their own initiative, have begun going through their own foster care caseloads to see if there are children who should be legally freed for adoption. One of those places is Los Angeles County, California. The Los Angeles effort began in 1970. Between 1970 and 1972 almost 800 children were freed for adoption. And almost 70 percent of the children were freed by relinquishment of the parents rather than by court action. By the end of 1972, over 350 of the 800 children had been placed in adoptive homes.[14]

The children accepted for adoptive planning ranged in age from infants to teenagers; most (70 percent) were under 6 years. Foster parents proved an important resource as adoptive parents, with almost one-third of the children being adopted by their foster parents. In many instances the child had been with the foster parents for many years, but the foster parents had not realized that adoption was possible.

From a foster care caseload of over 15,000 children, the adoption unit of Los Angeles County, once the program was set up, was receiving referrals of over 100 children a month.[15]

In a large-scale effort to find adoptable children in foster care caseloads, there is always the risk that some children who should be returned to their natural parents will be put up for adoption instead. But without such effort, the other error is being made—that of leaving large numbers of children to the vagaries of foster care when they could have the security of a permanent home.

It may seem contradictory, on the one hand, to be concerned about children growing up in foster homes and, on the other, to be enthusiastic about foster parents adopting the children who live with them. Yet it is not. Adoption brings with it a commitment and feeling of permanence. If the family moves to another state, the adopted child moves with them; a foster child probably will not. There is no anxiety that the birth parent will appear and take the child away.

The story of Maria, a Puerto Rican child caught in the New York foster care system, reveals the problems that can arise.

> Maria was born in June 1963 to a drug-addicted mother. She was placed in a nursery for a year.
>
> At age 1 she was placed in a Hispanic foster boarding home. At age 4 the foster parents expressed a willingness to adopt Maria, and a psychological examination found her mental development well within the average range.
>
> Maria's biological mother was in prison during 1966 but did not visit Maria until 1970 when Maria was 7 years old. After a few visits by her birth mother and other relatives, Maria became a very nervous child, constantly threatened by the fear that one day she would be taken away by her relatives. She had to repeat the first grade.
>
> The foster parents continued to wish to adopt Maria. The social worker told them that would not be possible unless the mother relinquished the child. [In view of the fact that abandonment and permanent neglect statutes of New York State provide a means to terminate parental rights via court action, this was a very misleading statement.]
>
> Maria developed further emotional problems. She was first seen by a psychiatric social worker for weekly therapy sessions beginning at age 12. At age 12 she was also freed for adoption. And, as the case record notes, Maria "can't wait to be adopted by her foster mother so that she can feel much more secure."
>
> At age 13, Maria was still waiting for a subsidized adoption to be completed.[16]

There are no easy answers. Many birth parents can be good parents once a crisis is over, and foster care provides one way of helping out during that crisis. Other birth parents seem to hold little potential for raising their children. It is children of these parents who should be considered as candidates for adoption. Right now these children are being left in limbo.

A 1977 study of children in foster care in New York City illustrates the problems of foster care. Of the 171 youngsters studied, only 4 percent entered foster care with severe social or emotional problems. After being in foster care, almost 20 percent deteriorated markedly. They developed severe anxiety, chronic bedwetting, constant nightmares, or severe hyperactivity. The longer the children were in foster care, the more likely they were to have severe problems. Also there was a clear relationship between the number of placements and social and emotional deterioration during placement. The more placements there were, the more likely the child was to have problems. The average American foster child lives in three foster homes.[17]

Given the shortage of adoptable babies, the foster care system has been one place to look for adoptable children. The fit between people wanting to adopt and the children needing adoption has not been all that close. Many of the children available for adoption through the foster care system have been older black children. Many of the people wanting to adopt have been whites seeking younger white children. Sometimes the whites did end up adopting a black child. However, the small social movement of whites adopting black children began before the shortage of white babies and slowed down while the shortage of white babies continued. The reasons for this pattern are discussed in chapter 6.

Adoption Exchanges—Local and International

In order to deal with problems of oversupply or undersupply of particular types of children at different agencies, adoption exchanges have been created. An agency with a child for which it has no home can list the child on an exchange, hoping that another agency will have an approved adopter who wants such a child. Exchanges sound better in theory than they have sometimes proved in practice. The effectiveness of an exchange rests primarily on the assumption that social workers in different agencies will have confidence in one another's competence. If a social worker in one agency says a prospective adopter will be a good parent, will the social worker in another agency accept that judgment? Agency rules get in the way also. If the agency with the child insists the adopter must be of a particular religion or age or income, some people who would be good parents are immediately disqualified. And, in fact, one of the reasons the agency had a surplus of children in the first place might be the agency's unrealistic expectations for adopters.[18]

Another impediment to the use of adoption exchanges is fees. It takes relatively little money to recruit adopters for babies and toddlers. So, in the days when such children were in oversupply, agencies with approved applicants were content just to get the child from the other agency and the fee from the adopters. Recruiting adopters for older children, however, takes much more time and money. One effective way for agencies which focus on the older child to finance themselves is by the placement fee from the agency providing the child. Unfortunately, a number of agencies with available children find it difficult to make such payments. It is often easier to pay thousands every year in foster care payments until the child becomes of age than to pay a fee once to an agency providing an adoptive family. It is possible, however, to finance such placement fees through the federal foster care system, and such payments have been worked out with the public agencies in Michigan, New Jersey, New York, and perhaps other states as well.[19]

Another difficulty with exchanges is that United Fund organizations are sometimes unwilling to support agencies which secure children from outside their area. Sometimes even getting the child from another agency within the United Fund's territory will disadvantage an agency from a budgetary point of view.

Unable to get children through their local agencies or through exchanges, some whites have sought children in foreign countries. International adoptions began with the homeless children generated by the Korean war and its aftermath. More international adoptions were fostered by the war in Vietnam. Some of the adopted children had had American fathers, either white or black, and so were less welcome in their mother's country than they would have been if they had only one racial heritage.

The birth parents have not always welcomed these international adoptions. In the panic at the end of the Vietnam war, in desperation some Vietnamese parents gave up their children for adoption, but once the parents were established in the United States, they tried very hard to get their children back.

In recent years, the importation of Vietnamese children has fallen while the number of children brought in from some Latin American countries has grown. Between 1968 and 1976 foreign adoptions more than quadrupled, going from 1612 to 6550.[20]

Independent Adoptions

For those whites who have been sure they wanted a white infant and have been willing to pay the price, white infants have been available through independent adoptions. These are adoptions where arrangements are made privately by a lawyer or other intermediary. The adopting parents have paid fees of $8000 to $10,000 and more. There can be a financial advantage to the expectant white mother of placing her baby through a lawyer or other intermediary. While pregnant, she can get her living and medical expenses paid by the attorney. The disadvantage, of course, is that she has to trust the judgment of the attorney to not put her baby in a harmful situation.[21]

What happens in those independent adoptions if the father of the white woman's baby is black? Not telling the lawyer, a white mother in New York was able to have her expenses paid. The adopting parents took the baby, assuming it was white. A few months later it became apparent that the baby's father had been black. The couple gave the child back to the lawyer, and he

reimbursed them for everything except hospital costs.[22] One wonders what
happened to the baby.

The change in the legal status of abortion in the United States has led to a
sharp decline in the number of babies becoming available for adoption. Adoption workers talk much more about finding homes for the older child. Some
agencies have shifted their resources in this direction. And it is true that whenever one reads descriptions of children available for adoption, whether the
children are listed on one of the state exchanges or on the Adoption Resource
Exchange of North America, the children are not infants or preschoolers.
There is definitely a need for adoptive homes for older children. But it would
be quite erroneous to assume that most of the children now being adopted are
older. Between 1969 and 1975, the adoption of children ages 6 and over rose
from 2 to 12 percent of all adoptions by unrelated persons. This is certainly a
significant increase. But equally significant is that, for the present, the vast
majority of adoptions by unrelated persons still involve babies under 1 year or
preschool youngsters (table 1-4).

Table 1-4
Percentage of Children Adopted by Unrelated Persons, by Age, 1969, 1974
and 1975

	Agency and Independent Adoptions			Agency Adoptions Only
Age of Children	1975[a]	1974[b]	1969[c]	1969[c]
Under 1 year	64	70	87	87
1 to 5	24	21	11	11
6 to 11	10	8	2	2
12 and over	2	1	d	d
All ages	100	100	100	100

Source: U.S. Department of Health, Education, and Welfare, *Adoptions in 1975,* April
1977, p. 15; *Adoptions in 1974,* April 1976, p. 16; *Adoptions in 1969,* undated, p. 10.

[a]Based on reports on 27,142 children in 34 states.

[b]Based on reports on 25,872 children in 33 states.

[c]Based on reports from 38 states.

[d]Less than 0.5 percent.

Black Adopters Can Be Found

With black children of all ages needing adoptive homes, the question arises of whether black adoptive families can be found. In the 1960s the research related to black adoptions seemed to answer no. Several small studies surveyed blacks in particular cities and found that they were not much interested in adoption. Later, however, other research showed that if whites in the general population are surveyed, very few of them are interested in adopting either. Yet agency personnel were agreed that there were enough white adoptive applicants.[23] The flaw in the survey approach then became apparent. All the studies had assumed that potential adopters, a very small portion of the population, could be found by using general survey methods. Potential adopters could not be found in this way.

The way to assess whether more blacks are interested in adopting is to look at those instances where effective recruitment policies have been followed and to see what has happened. In some instances, the results have been impressive. Between 1967 and 1971, black placements at the Baltimore City Department of Social Services increased from 9 to almost 80.[24] In the mid-1970s the Child Adoption Counseling and Referral Program of New York, after careful screening and evaluation, was able to find 60 prospective black adoptive parents in a year.[25] In 1969, Homes for Black Children in Detroit, a new agency, placed 100 black children in its first nine months of operation.[26]

The immediate success of these efforts is understandable when we pause to consider black history, for black families have a remarkable story in what they have done for grandchildren, nieces and nephews, and children not related to the family at all. Families who have sometimes not had enough for themselves have nevertheless accepted responsibility for an extra child.[27] A child was there and needed a home; someone would provide it.

With such a tradition, it is not surprising that agencies which follow appropriate policies can find dozens of blacks who want to adopt a child. The first step for the agencies is a commitment to finding black adopters.

Notes

1. Greater Washington Area Council on Adoptable Children, *Newsletter*, March and April 1978. Available from Gary and Jean Shapiro, 1813 Glendora Drive, District Heights, Maryland 20028. Reprinted with permission.

2. Joseph Morgenstern, "The New Face of Adoption," *Newsweek* September 13, 1971, p. 66. Elizabeth Herzog, Cecelia Sudia, Jane Harwood, and Carol Newcomb, *Families for Black Children* (Washington: Government Printing Office, 1971), p. 67. Sheila K. Johnson, "The Business in Babies," *New York Times Magazine* October 17, 1975, p. 11.

3. *Opportunity*, Annual newsletter on black adoptions, published at 2301 N.W. Glisan Street, Portland, Oregon 97210.

4. Dawn Day Wachtel, "Options of the Single Pregnant Woman," *Review of Radical Political Economics* 4, no. 3 (July 1972): 86-107. Leslie A. Westoff, "Parent and Child: Kids with Kids," *New York Times Magazine* February 22, 1976, pp. 14-15, 63-65. Enid Nemy, "Pregnant and Single, and Glad to Be Both," *New York Times* March 5, 1971, p. 20.

5. Lucille J. Grow, "A New Look at Supply and Demand in Adoption," report from the Child Welfare League of America, May 1970, p. 8; and Barbara L. Haring, *Adoption Statistics* (New York: Child Welfare League of America, May 1976), pp. 2, 6, 15.

6. Betty Medsger, "Agency Changes Policy on Adoption," *Washington Post* January 20, 1973.

7. Personal interviews with the social worker at the referral service and with agency supervisors at each of the twenty-four Washington, D.C., and Baltimore adoption agencies, completed in 1970.

8. Rose Bernstein, *Helping Unmarried Mothers* (New York: Association Press, 1971). Elizabeth A. Lawder et al., *A Study of Black Adoption Families: A Comparison of a Traditional and a Quasi-Adoption Program* (New York: Child Welfare League of America, 1971). Zitha Turitz, *A New Look at Adoption* (New York: Council on Social Work Education, 1969), p. 67. Andrew Billingsley, *Black Families in White America* (Englewood Cliffs, N.J.: Prentice-Hall, 1968), p. 162. Margaret Boothby, "Child Welfare Services for Black Children," *Child Welfare* March 1969, p. 170. Walter A. Heath, "Mass Communication Methods in Recruiting Minority Group Adoptive Homes," *Public Welfare* July 1955, p. 114. Clarence D. Fischer, "Homes for Black Children," *Child Welfare* February 1971, p. 108.

9. Edward A. Duffy, *The Effect of Changes in the State Abortion Laws* (Washington: Government Printing Office, 1971), pp. 1-3. E. Boyd Steele, "Abortion Laws" (Washington: Women's Bureau, U.S. Department of Labor, May 1970), pp. 1-6.

10. Dawn Day Wachtel, "Options of the Single Pregnant Woman: Legal Abortions Rose by 11% in 1975," *New York Times* May 16, 1976.

11. Lucille J. Grow and Michael J. Smith, "Adoption Trends: 1969-1970," *Child Welfare* July 1971, p. 404.

12. "Adoptive Homes Needed in San Antonio, Texas," *Adoptalk*, Second Quarter 1978, p. 16. Laura Foreman, "President Defends Court's Action Curbing Federal Aid for Abortions," *New York Times* July 13, 1977. Lesley Oelsner, "Court Rules States May Deny Medicaid for Some Abortions," *New York Times* June 21, 1977. Martin Tolchin, "Compromise Is Voted by House and Senate in Abortion Dispute," *New York Times* December 8, 1977.

13. Cynthia Stokes, "Editor's Page: Abortion and Adoption," *Child Welfare* December 1970, p. 544.

14. Mary M. O'Neill, "Adoption: Identification and Service," *Child Welfare* May 1972, pp. 314-317.

15. Ibid.

16. Office of the Comptroller, City of New York, "The Children are Waiting: The Failure to Achieve Permanent Homes for Foster Children in New York City," May 1977, p. 10-11. Reprinted by Permission.

17. Ibid. Tom Wicker, "Fragmenting Children," *New York Times* May 8, 1977, p. 19E.

18. Elizabeth Herzog, Cecelia Sudia, Jane Harwood, and Carol Newcomb, *Families for Black Children: The Search for Adoptive Parents, An Experience Survey* (Washington: Government Printing Office, 1971), p. 9; and Joyce A. Ladner, *Mixed Families* (Garden City, N.Y.: Anchor Press, 1977), p. 59.

19. Peter Kihss, "Drive Will Seek Adoptive Parents for Many Black Foster Children," *New York Times* June 19, 1977, p. 39. Jo Steele, "Purchase of Service," *Arena News* September 1977, p. 6.

20. Louise Saul, "Milltown Parents Find a Son," *New York Times* July 3, 1977; "An Outline of the Holt Adoption Program Annual Report 1969," *National Adoptalk* September-October 1971, p. 6; and Wendell Rawls, "Adoption Abroad Brings Heartache to Some Couples," *New York Times* June 24, 1978.

21. Mary Breasted, "Baby Brokers Reaping Huge Fees," *New York Times* June 28, 1977. Joseph F. Sullivan, "Adoption Lawyer, Facing Charges, Is Cleared for State-Run Program," *New York Times* December 10, 1977. Sheila K. Johnson, "The Business in Babies," *New York Times Magazine* August 17, 1975, p. 65.

22. Breasted, ibid., p. 11.

23. L.C. Deasy and Olive W. Quinn, "The Urban Negro and Adoption of Children," *Child Welfare* November 1962, pp. 400-407; Irving A. Fowler, "The Urban Middle-Class Negro and Adoption: Two Series of Studies and Their Implications for Action," *Child Welfare* November 1966, pp. 522-525. L.C. Deasy and J.W. Mullaney, "The Suburban White and the Adoption of Children," *Social Science Review* September 1970, pp. 275-284. Gwendolyn Foote and Roseland L. Putnam, *Negro Attitudes Toward Adoption in Hartford* (New Haven: Connecticut Child Welfare Association, 1966).

24. Edmond D. Jones, "On Transracial Adoption of Black Children," *Child Welfare* March 1972, p. 161.

25. Personal communication from Leora Neal, director of the Child Adoption Counseling and Referral Program, New York.

26. Clarence D. Fischer, "Homes for Black Children," *Child Welfare* February 1971, pp. 108-111.

27. Herzog et al., *Families for Black Children*, p. 54.

2

Finding Black Homes

The word "adoption" conjures up the happy image of two parents and their new baby, delighted with each other and with themselves. The charm of the picture is the same whether the new family is black or white.

One might think that adoption agencies and their social workers would be equally happy to produce either family group. But this is not so. A study of 24 adoption agencies in the District of Columbia and Baltimore metropolitan areas done in the early 1970s illustrates the existence of agency policies which explicitly excluded blacks, the negative attitudes of some social workers toward blacks, and the practices followed by some agencies which discouraged black adopters. On the positive side, the study also identified successful techniques used by agencies and social workers who were willing to make black adoptions.[1]

Of the 24 agencies, 18 were small parts of larger social welfare bureaucracies providing a wide variety of social work services. In these large organizations, only those employees involved in adoptive placement decisions were included in the study. This group embraced workers who counseled mothers considering giving up a child, those whose main focus was foster care, and those involved with adoptive applicants.

Data on agency policy were collected through personal interviews with the 32 relevant supervisors. Data on the behavior of individual social workers and their interpretations of policy were acquired through 272 self-administered questionnaires.[2]

The need for more black adopters was overwhelming. More black children had been relinquished and were awaiting adoptive homes in 1970 than had been adopted in the entire previous year. Although the situation sounds very bad, and it was, at least by 1970 some agencies were placing black children. In the early 1960s, none of the agencies had been very involved with black adopters. The few who did change during the 1960s probably did so in response to the ideology and influence of the civil rights movement.

Outside Pressures

It is possible to identify three citizens' groups with a civil rights flavor in the two metropolitan areas which were concerned with child welfare and black adoptions during the 1960s. In the District of Columbia, there was a group called For Love of Children (FLOC) which focused primarily on the problems of Junior

Village, an institutional home for children. Another group, the Council on Adoptable Children, was made up primarily of whites who had adopted across racial lines. In Baltimore, Delta Sigma Theta sorority, a black professional women's group, concerned itself with black adoptions by helping organize a media campaign and by providing volunteers to staff a 24-hour hot-line to answer inquiries from blacks responding to mass media publicity.[3] With their various approaches, these groups created a gentle push toward more agency involvement with black adoptions. Even so, by 1969, at a time when a quarter of the Washington, D.C., and Baltimore metropolitan area populations were black, only 5 of the 24 agencies were making 14 percent or more of their placements with black adopters (table 2-1).

Between 1969 and 1971, three events enhanced the efforts of these three groups. The first was a change in the legal status of abortion in the District of Columbia and Maryland and a little later in Virginia. The supply of white babies dropped precipitously.

Second, the funding situation changed. The United Givers Fund (UGF) in the District of Columbia pledged to "reorient agency priorities to better serve the black community;" black support was withdrawn from UGF; and a United Black Fund was created. (The United Black Fund was created because agencies were not serving the black population. In an effort to reform UGF, the United Black Fund demanded that agencies seeking UGF funds for the first time be examined to see if they were meeting pressing community needs.) One of the adoption agencies included in this study was seeking UGF funding for the first time and consequently was under particular pressure to show it could serve the

Table 2-1
Agency Involvement with Black Adopters, Washington, D.C., and Baltimore, 1969 and 1971[a]

Percentage of Placements with Black Adopters	Number of Agencies (Percentage of Agencies)	
	1969[b]	1971
Less than 6 percent	15 (63)	8 (33)
7 to 13 percent	3 (13)	6 (25)
14 percent and over	6 (25)	10 (42)
Total	24 (100)	24 (100)

Source: District of Columbia and Baltimore Adoption Agency Survey.

[a]The data are for different periods. For some agencies the statistical year was March to February; for others, June to May; and so on.

[b]The placement figures for one agency are from 1970.

black population. However, all the UGF agencies felt this pressure to some extent.[4]

Finally, the Stern Community Law Firm was created. This public interest law firm advertised free legal assistance to any District of Columbia resident who wished to adopt a child and who was refused because she or he was single, over 45, of a different race or religion than the child, a foster parent, or a couple planning for both adoptive parents to continue working.[5]

The result of all these pressures on agencies was that between 1969 and 1971 adoptions by blacks increased impressively: 17 of the 24 agencies increased the proportion of their placements with black adopters. Only 2 of the 24 showed a decline.

Although the pressures from outside the agencies were a powerful motivation for change, not all the agencies were equally receptive. Some were staffed by people who wanted to involve their agencies more in black adoptions; others were staffed by people who did not care or were opposed. Policy on black adoptions, as set by the agency's board, also played a role. Finally, given a favorable policy, an agency, in order to succeed, had to follow practices which would attract black applicants and encourage them to continue through the adoption process.

Policy and Attitudes on Black Adoptions

The first step toward black adoptions was having a policy which would permit such placements to be made. In 1970, supervisors in the 24 adoption agencies in the District of Columbia and Baltimore were asked this question: "Does this agency have a policy which permits placing black children with black families?" Four supervisors reported that their agency policies did *not* permit the placement of black children with black adopters. One of these four agencies was so small that it could not reasonably be expected to be involved in black adoptions. The agency consisted of only one part-time social worker who approved one or two American Greek Orthodox adoptive couples a year. The couples then went to Greece to adopt a child there. The social worker's salary was covered by fees and contributions from the church.

The remaining three agencies which had policies against black adopters were larger and focused on the American scene, with perhaps an occasional international adoption. These three agencies could have been expected to concern themselves with black adopters. They did not. Consistent with their policies, these agencies made virtually no placements with black adopters between 1969 and 1971.[6]

Two of these three agencies were sponsored by religious organizations whose congregations did not include blacks. Both of the sectarian agencies received government funds for part of their program costs. The third agency was a private, nonsectarian agency which operated entirely on nongovern-mental funds.

These agencies were licensed by one or more of the three political jurisdic-tions involved in this study—the District of Columbia, Maryland, and Virginia. (The Virginia agencies were located in the suburban counties adjacent to the District of Columbia.) At the time of this study, the licensing organizations were making no effort to encourage a policy of nondiscrimination, through either the withdrawal or the suspension of a license. The four agencies which refused to make placements with black adopters together accounted for 100 adoptions in 1969. This represented about 5 percent of the placements of children of all races made by the 24 agencies in that year.

The remaining 20 agencies in the Washington and Baltimore metropolitan areas did not officially prohibit placements with black adopters, but they did vary considerably in the extent to which their own employees saw the agency as a receptive place for a black person. Social workers were asked whether they would recommend their own agency to a black friend interested in adoption. When all the social workers at an agency were willing to recommend their own agency to black friends, a favorable reception to black applicants seemed ensured. This positive situation occurred at 11 agencies, which together averaged 23 percent of their placements with black adopters in 1969 and 30 percent in 1971. At the remaining 9 agencies, social worker attitudes were unfavorable. The results were unfavorable also. In 1969 these 9 agencies averaged 3 percent of their placements with blacks. By 1971, the figure had grown to only 8 percent (table 2-2).

An agency policy which explicitly prohibits black adoptions is probably illegal; but until it is challenged, it is easy to pursue. Black applicants simply can be turned away.

What about agencies which do not prohibit black adoptions? Why do they differ? Part of the answer has already been suggested. It lies with staff and the attitudes with which they approach black applicants. Part of the answer also lies in agency practices. Whether intentional or not, some practices encourage and others discourage black adopters.

People Telling People

An agency's reputation is created as applicants talk to their friends who in turn talk to their friends. Religious leaders, physicians, and others whose professional lives bring them in touch with people who want to adopt also play a role. To understand the importance of personal contacts, consider the matter from the viewpoint of the person applying to adopt. How does a person choose to adopt? How does a person choose a particular agency?

Table 2-2
Agency Policy and Worker Attitudes Toward Black Adopters, by Percentage of
Agency Placements Made with Black Adopters, Washington, D.C., and Baltimore,
1969 and 1971

Policy and Workers' Attitudes in 1969	Number of Agencies	Black Placements as a Percentage of Total[a]	
		1969	1971
Policy against black adoptions	4	0	1
Policy permits black adoptions[b]			
Social workers discourage	9	3	8
Social workers favor	11	23	30
All agencies	24	12[c]	17

Source: District of Columbia and Baltimore Adoption Agency Survey.

[a]Average of agency percentages.

[b]If virtually all (98 percent or more) of the social workers at an agency were willing to
recommend their own agency to black friends, the social workers were said to *favor* black
adopters at their agency; if less than 98 percent were willing to refer black adopters to their
own agency, then the social workers were said to *discourage* black adopters at their own
agency.
    The issue was posed to social workers as follows: "If some friends of yours, a white
couple, wanted to adopt, what agency in this area would you suggest they apply to?" and
"If some friends of yours, a black couple, wanted to adopt, what agency in this area would
you suggest they apply to?" If black friends were encouraged to apply, the question on
white friends was irrelevant. If black friends were discouraged and white friends encouraged,
social workers were coded as discouraging black adopters. In a few cases, both black and
white friends were discouraged from applying. Taking the most favorable interpretation possible of such answers, the social worker was coded as favoring black adopters at her agency
but just being reluctant to encourage either black or white friends because she did not want
to deal with their disappointment in case they were turned down.

[c]The placement figure for one agency is from 1970.

    Consulting those they know, the prospective adopters learn the pros and
cons of adoption and something about the various adoption agencies in their
area. On the basis of this information (and having been coached on what to say
and how the agency works), prospective adopters make their initial contact with
the agency.
    Both supervisors and social workers in the study agencies were aware of the
importance of personal recommendations. Of 24 supervisors, 23 reported some
type of personal contact as the most important referral source for adoptive
applicants at their agency. For most, the referral source was other adoptive
applicants. For the remainder it was religious leaders or physicians.
    Social workers were asked whether they agreed with the following: "For
this agency, the most important referral source of qualified adoptive applicants

is couples who have already adopted through the agency." At 20 agencies there were sufficient responses for analysis, and at 17 of these 20 the majority of social workers agreed with the statement. In her study of adoption agencies in the New York area, Bradley also found that informal referrals played an important role in the person's decision to apply to a particular agency.[7]

From the point of view of the adoption agency, the informal referral system is often quite advantageous.[8] Some would-be adopters who might not meet the agency's standards have already learned this and eliminated themselves. They have never applied, and consequently a social worker has been spared the unpleasant task of rejecting them.

Those who do apply already know something of how the agency works, so the social worker has to spend less time explaining. Having learned some of the issues the social workers will raise, the applicants have already considered these issues and found their own solutions or learned answers used previously by successful applicants. A social worker wants sincere answers, but she or he is not ungrateful when applicants are ready to adopt and the worker is freed from spending time helping the applicants think through the issues.

The informal referral system is not without its disadvantages. The information may be out of date. The information may not reach the people whom the agency most needs to apply. This would appear to be the case with the adoption agencies which in the past have been involved almost exclusively with white adopters and now desire to begin placing black children with black adopters.

If race were not a factor, informal referrals would bring in blacks and whites in rough proportion to the childless population interested in adopting.[9] But race is a factor in American society. Slavery existed until the Civil War. Beginning in the 1890s, segregation was made legal under the myth of "separate but equal." In 1968 the Kerner commission reported that "To continue present policies is to make permanent the division of our country into two societies . . . ."[10] Commenting on the Kerner commission report, Andrew Billingsley pointed out the obvious: "We have and have always had two separate and unequal societies. What is new is a recognition on the part of the white society that these two societies exist and a determination on the part of black society that they should no longer exist."[11]

Suggestive of the social division between blacks and whites on the individual level is a study by Laumann of 1013 white men living in the Detroit metropolitan area. Of the 3035 friends reported by this group, 2 were black.[12]

Religious organizations remain largely segregated also, so that a religious leader referring members of his or her own congregation is likely to send persons of only one race.

All this suggests that an agency which has had a white clientele in the past will have to depart from business-as-usual in order to attract black adopters.

Reaching Out

In the early 1960s, all the agencies in Washington and Baltimore were basically white adoption agencies. The steps some agencies took to increase their ties with the black community were grounded not in theory but in trial and error. To whatever extent it was used, the social work literature offered some useful guidance. Some writers stressed the need for publicity: newspapers; radio and television, particularly programs with black audiences; bus and streetcar posters; talks at professional, church, or fraternal groups; and reaching out to blacks who adopted previously.[13]

Litwak and Meyer have developed a typology of the techniques that organizations like adoption agencies can use to reach out to black people or any other target group.[14] The techniques include, sending a professional worker into the target neighborhood, setting up an office in the target neighborhood, reaching out through local community leaders, working with local community organizations, asking for assistance from persons who have ties with both the agency and the neighborhood, and utilizing a variety of mass-media techniques.

Using this typology, an index of adoption agency outreach to the black community was developed. Agencies in the District of Columbia and Baltimore were given 1 point for use of each of the following techniques within the previous two years:

1. Assigning someone from the agency the responsibility of going out and recruiting black adopters[15]
2. Having an office in a black or an integrated neighborhood[16]
3. Asking for referrals from black community leaders such as ministers or civil rights activists[17]
4. Asking assistance from organizations such as the Urban League which have close ties with the black community[18]
5. Asking black adopters to refer interested friends[19]
6. Publicizing the need for black adopters through the general media[20]
7. Publicizing the need for black adopters through media specifically directed toward the black community[21]

Agency scores on this index could, and did, vary from 0 to 7.

The agencies used the outreach techniques in a variety of ways. In Washington, D.C., several agencies took advantage of an offer of free time given by a local television station; other specific techniques appeared to have been initiated by the agencies themselves. In Baltimore, the impetus for the outreach techniques came through the combined efforts of Delta Sigma Theta sorority, a black professional women's service group, and the Maryland State Conference on Social Welfare.

Agency outreach did make a difference. Three-quarters of the agencies with low outreach scores were low in their involvement with black adopters, while three-quarters of the agencies with high outreach scores were high in black placements (table 2–3).

Agency personnel were not equally enthusiastic about all the outreach techniques. Mass-media publicity was particularly unpopular with some social workers. Mass-media publicity did take a lot of time per completed adoption. Some applicants were not serious; they had not thought the matter through. Responding to the picture of an appealing child, they impulsively called the agency. Upon reflection, they realized that they did not wish to adopt at that time, and they dropped out. In such cases some social workers felt their time had been wasted. Other workers took a broader view, realizing that each conversation was a small contribution to educating the black public on adoption.

The more serious applicants brought in by mass-media publicity required more social worker time as well. This was so because these applicants had not had the advantage of the coaching that the informal referral system provided. These applicants did not know what questions the social worker was going to ask, so they had not had time to think through the answers. Also, they had not learned the answers that had worked for other applicants to that agency.

Five agencies had kept records on the number of inquiries handled and placements made as a result of mass-media publicity. Most successful was a public agency which made 3 adoptions after processing 16 inquiries—almost a 20 percent success rate. The worst performance was by an agency which made no placements at all after receiving 50 inquiries.

The attitudes and qualifications of the applicants are only a partial explanation of why some applicants finally adopt and others do not. Qualified, serious black applicants can be driven away by unfavorable social worker attitudes and inappropriate agency procedures.

Sympathetic Processing

Traditionally, white-oriented agencies—as all the study agencies were—cannot assume that black applicants will approach the agency with trust. Black applicants are suspicious.[22] The very fact that the agency has had little contact with the black community raises the question in the black applicant's mind about the sincerity of the agency's professed desire to encourage black adopters.

How can the agency assure black applicants of fair treatment? One important way is to handle the initial inquiry immediately.[23] Once the applicant applies, the social worker should not delay, but should follow through on the study as rapidly as possible. Although not intended that way, delays may well be interpreted by the black applicant as a message of rejection. Delays have often

Table 2-3
**Agency Characteristics in 1970, by Percentage of Placements with Black
Adopters in 1971, Washington, D.C., and Baltimore**

Agency Characteristics in 1970	Number of Agencies	Percentage of Placements with Black Adopters in 1971		
		Total	Less than 14	14 or More
All agencies	20	100	50	50
Workers' attitude toward black adopters[a]				
Favorable	9	100	0	100
Unenthusiastic	7	100	86	14
Negative	4	100	100	0
Outreach				
Low (Index score 0 to 4)	11	100	73	27
High (Index score 5 to 7)	9	100	22	78
Sympathetic processing				
Low (Index score 0 to 3)	10	100	80	20
High (Index score 4 to 6)	10	100	20	80
Percentage of black social workers on staff				
None	11	100	64	36
1 or more	9	100	33	67
Number of professionals[b]				
1 to 6	6	100	17	83
7 to 12	7	100	71	29
16 to 75[c]	7	100	57	43
Total professional time per week[b]				
Less than 200 hours	10	100	30	70
200 or more	10	100	70	30
Percentage of blacks in territory served[d]				
Low (14 percent or less)	10	100	80	20
High (more than 14 percent)	10	100	30	70
Agency sponsorship				
Public	9	100	56	44
Private, nonsecular	5	100	40	60
Private, religious	6	100	50	50
Proportion of agency funds from community source[e]				
90 to 100 percent[c]	10	100	60	40
15 to 75 percent	7	100	57	43
None	3	100	0	100

Source: District of Columbia and Baltimore Adoption Agency Survey.

[a]The percentage of social workers who would refer black friends to their own agency was
98 to 100 percent for favorable agencies, 75 to 91 percent for unenthusiastic, and 33 to 70
percent for negative.

Table 2-3 continued

[b]Almost one-fourth of all social workers worked part time.

[c]The gap or gaps between groups of numbers occur because no agencies reported characteristics falling into those ranges.

[d]When an agency had two or more definitions of domain with respect to adoptive applicants, the domain which included all groups was used. This was done because the domain mentioned for a special group (such as blacks) usually was left undefined. A supervisor might say, for example, that the primary domain of the agency was the local county for both whites and blacks, but that blacks residing outside the county would also be considered if a child were available.

[e]Agency here refers to the wider organization of which many adoption agencies were only a part. Funding for the entire organization is an appropriate indicator here because the antidiscrimination laws require that an organization receiving government funds not discriminate in any of its activities. Expenditures solely on adoption activities were not available in any case for multipurpose agencies.

been part of a subtle process of racial discrimination which black applicants have experienced many times before.

Items on the application itself can have an adverse impact. For example, does the agency form inquire about race? Think of it this way: adoption is one of the few activities where race is an appropriate consideration. An application with space for national origin (illustrated by such examples as English, French, or German) was probably not designed with black applicants in mind—at least it will seem so to the black applicant. After all, as Americans use the term, nationality refers to differences among white ethnic groups.

An agency policy against two working parents can also exclude excellent potential adopters. Many women, both black and white, prefer or need to work. Many black families have achieved middle-class income levels only through having two incomes. If the wife or husband stopped working, the family would suffer real hardships—and for no reason. It is quite possible for working mothers and fathers to arrange for good child care at times when they must be away.[24] Many of the social workers in this study should have known this from personal experience; over 60 percent had children living at home!

The timing of appointments is important. Many working people find it difficult to take time off from work without losing pay. If agency staff are willing to make appointments on evenings and Saturdays, adoption by working people will be facilitated.[25]

Extensive fertility testing is also inappropriate. It is time-consuming and expensive.[26] Both the time and the expense involved can cause unnecessary dropouts in the application process. Sophisticated agencies are now willing to accept the applicants' judgment. If the couple wants a child and feels they can

love an adopted child, that is enough. The couple needs only to have thought
the matter through and to feel that if they later happen to produce a child, they
will still love the adopted child. Adopting couples occasionally have children
later anyway, even with fertility testing. (For couples who can have children
but who choose to adopt anyway, fertility testing is irrelevant.)

Whether by requiring fertility testing or charging an adoption fee, an
agency requirement that keeps adoption costs high discourages some qualified
black applicants. By keeping adoption costs low, agencies can encourage more
black applicants.[27]

To test whether an agency's practices were encouraging to black adopters,
an index of sympathetic processing was created. An agency was given a point
for each of the following:

1. Speed in response to the initial inquiry. The supervisor reported that either
    the agency processed applicants for the hard-to-place child faster than
    applicants for other children or all applicants were seen within four months
    of the initial inquiry.
2. Speed in processing. The supervisor reported that it usually took less than
    six months between the first interview with an applicant and placement of
    a child.
3. A question on race as well as nationality on the application. An agency was
    also given a point if the application form did not mention either race or
    nationality, because when the issue is not raised at all, the black applicant
    would have no reason to feel excluded.
4. Adoption by working parents permitted. At least 50 percent of the social
    workers reported they often made placements with black working mothers,
    or a supervisor reported that agency policy permitted adoption by working
    mothers. (The latter was used only in those few instances when the response
    rate for social workers at the agency was low.)
5. Interviewing applicants on evenings and Saturdays.
6. Fertility testing not required. At least 40 percent of social workers re-
    ported they made placements with couples who were biologically capable
    of having their own children, or a supervisor reported that agency policy
    permitted adoptions by couples capable of having their own children.
    (Supervisor reports were used only in those few instances when the response
    rate from the agency social workers was low.)
7. No fee charged for adoption.

Agency scores on this index varied from 0 to 6. As had been anticipated,
agencies with high scores on sympathetic processing were very involved with
black adopters while agencies with low scores were doing little with black
adopters (table 2-3).

It should be pointed out that sympathetic processing would be attractive to

white applicants as well as to black. White people do not like to have to take
time off from work if they will be penalized for it. Whites are not enthusiastic
about long waits as they apply to adopt a child. If both spouses are working,
a white woman or man may be as unenthusiastic about quitting as a black
woman or man. The point is that the agencies have more white applicants
than they know what to do with. If qualified white applicants are turned off
and drop out in the process, no white infant goes without a home, although an
older white child may. For every qualified black applicant lost in the process,
it is certain that a black infant or older child will remain in a foster home.

Black Social Workers

The presence of black social workers at an agency could make a contribution
in several ways. They could serve as interpreters of black culture to white
social workers. They might have particularly good ideas about how to reach
out effectively into the black community to attract applicants. Also, they
might have insight into how agency processing could be improved so that qualified black applicants would not be driven off. Finally, the very presence of
black social workers at the agency would help convince black applicants that
the agency was concerned about providing service to black adopters.

In 1970, only about 15 percent of the social workers in the District of
Columbia and Baltimore metropolitan areas were black. They were not evenly
distributed among the 20 agencies which had a policy of placing with black
adopters; 11 agencies had no black staff at all. At the remaining 9 agencies,
the proportion of staff which was black varied from about 5 to 45 percent.

The black social workers did make a difference. Only a third of the
agencies with no black social workers were highly involved with black adopters
in 1971. Two-thirds of the agencies which hired black social workers were
highly involved (table 2-3).

Agency Size

One might think that both the outreach and sympathetic processing techniques
might require extra staff time and that agencies with large staffs would have an
advantage. Interestingly enough, this does not seem to be the case. The small
agencies were most involved with black adopters. This was true whether size
was measured in terms of the number of professionals or total professional
hours worked per week (table 2-3).[28]

Although all agencies perform essentially the same tasks, the time allocated
to each task can be very different. For example, an agency can spend staff
time counseling every pregnant woman who asks for help, or the agency can

restrict itself to those women who seem likely to give up a child for adoption. An agency can interview all applicants or only those who are asking for a type of child the agency has available.

In the District of Columbia, Virginia, and Maryland, privately funded agencies eventually turn over long-term foster care children to the public agencies, so it is the public agencies which eventually have the large numbers of children in foster care. Those agencies with large numbers of foster children devote much of their staff time to foster care supervision.

Agencies can also misuse their resources. As if to demonstrate this, after the change in the abortion laws, some agencies in Maryland and Virginia continued to do home studies on all persons applying to adopt regardless of whether the type of children desired was available. The waiting list for white infants at one agency reached 500 and at another 450.[29] At the time, these agencies were placing about 100 white children a year.

Altogether, agencies can distribute their resources in very different ways. Given this, it is perhaps not surprising that smaller agencies, if they choose to do so, can find the resources to seek out black adopters.

Agency Funding

What gives an agency the incentive to put resources into attracting black adopters? One answer could be the source of the agency's funds. In recent years it has become established in principle, if not in practice, that organizations funded by community sources are expected to serve all the population and not just certain segments of it. Adoption agencies can be recipients of two different kinds of community funds: those collected through taxes and those collected through voluntary contributions to a local United Givers Fund or Community Chest.

The nine public agencies in this study were supported entirely through tax dollars. Eight of the eleven private agencies were supported either by United Fund dollars or government tax money or both. The private agencies received government funds through direct grants for particular programs and through purchase-of-care arrangements for foster care. Under a typical purchase-of-care arrangement, the private agency locates the foster home and provides the social work supervision under contract with the public agency.

The expectation was that the larger the fraction of an agency's funding coming from community sources, the greater the imperative the agency staff would feel to locate black adopters. This does not seem to have been the case at all. In fact, all 3 of the 20 agencies which received *no* community funds were quite involved with black adopters, much more so than agencies who received even 90 or 100 percent of their monies from community sources (table 2-3). When public agencies were contrasted with private agencies, both religious and nonsectarian in sponsorship, no strong patterns were revealed. The private, non-

sectarian agencies showed only a slight tendency toward greater involvement
with black adopters than the other agencies (table 2-3).

Territory Served

All the agencies involved in this study were located in metropolitan Washington,
D.C., or Baltimore or had at least one of their branch offices located in these
two metropolitan areas in 1970. Both the District of Columbia and Baltimore
metropolitan areas were about 25 percent black at that time; yet the proportions
of black people living in the various agencies' territories were quite different.

This disparity occurred because the agencies had defined the territories and
populations to which they would give service quite differently. Some sectarian
agencies, for example, were willing to place children only with persons who were
members of their religious group. Others would place only within a broad
religious grouping, such as Protestant. One Catholic agency differentiated
according to how difficult it might be to place a particular child. An easy-to-
place child would always be placed with a Catholic family. A hard-to-place
child might be placed with any adopter who was willing to raise the child Catholic.

Public agencies also showed considerable variation in the territory served.
Some restricted their domains to the counties in which they were located. Others
were willing to go outside their county or state to find adopters, if the child was
hard to place or black. The more flexible agencies saw the child as their primary
client. As a resident of the county, that child was entitled to service, even if the
potential adopter came from outside the state or region. This same kind of
argument has been used by United Givers Fund agencies that make adoptive
placements outside the territory covered by their particular fund.

In some ways the flexibility of the agencies in terms of the black and hard-
to-place child worked to the advantage of black applicants. Blacks from more
distant locations could seek a child at these agencies. And when an agency used
mass-media publicity to blanket a whole area, black applicants would not be
turned away simply because they lived outside the agency's territory. But the
expansion of the agency's territory was not an unmixed blessing. This was so
because the tendency of agencies to expand their territories to include counties
which were largely white worked to reduce the importance of black clientele
at even the most black-oriented agencies. For example, in 1970 the population
of Baltimore City was 46 percent black, and the population of the District of
Columbia was 71 percent black. Yet because of the tendency of agencies
located in high-density black areas to extend their boundaries, no agency involved in this study had more than 29 percent of its territory black, and for
many agencies the figure was far lower.

For agencies with a purely geographical definition of domain, an estimate of the racial composition could be made by using 1970 census data. For the sectarian agencies, the estimate of the racial composition of their domain was made on the basis of information supplied by religious officials and other relevant data.

Since the racial composition of an agency's territory affects the proportion of potential black adopters, it seems likely that this factor also would influence the proportion of the agency's placements made with black adopters. This would be particularly true since there is some element of choice in an agency's domain—that is, by changing its boundaries, an agency can increase or decrease the proportion of its prospective clientele who are black. This expectation was borne out by the data. Agencies with a high proportion of blacks in their territory also made a relatively high proportion of their placements with black adopters. Similarly, agencies with a low proportion of blacks in their territories made a small proportion of their placements with black adopters (table 2-3).

Statistical Analysis

The main message of this chapter has been that an agency can effectively increase its placements with black adopters by utilizing a variety of outreach techniques, by being flexible and sensitive when processing black applicants, and by hiring black social workers. The cross tabulations presented in table 2-3 are useful starting points for looking at the relationship between two variables. The correlation coefficient, which can take into account the individual variations in pairs of items, is a more sensitive indicator. The interpretation of a correlation coefficient is fairly straightforward. A score of 1.00 means that when one factor increases or decreases, the other factor increases or decreases in the same way. A score of 0 means there is no relationship between the two factors in how they change. A score of .60 would mean that there was an important relationship between the two factors, but the changes in one were only partly associated with the changes in the other. By using this sensitive indicator, the factor most highly associated with agency placements with black adopters is the percentage of agency social workers who were black. The correlation coefficient is over .80 (table 2-4).

It had been expected that agency employment of black social workers would affect agency involvement in black adoptions. Yet the great strength of the association was a surprise. Upon consideration, however, it is quite understandable. Black social workers in an agency would probably inform and strengthen any agency efforts at increasing black adoptions. The black social workers might encourage publicity, and when an agency was considering various kinds of publicity, perhaps the black social worker would be most likely to suggest an effective means of doing this. A black social worker, in touch with black feelings, might be more likely to develop a publicity message which

Table 2-4
Correlation Matrix:[a] Relationships among Key Variables in Study Agencies, Washington, D.C., and Baltimore, 1970 and 1971

			Variable		
	1	2	3	4	5
1. 1970 black adopters[b]	–	.89	.56	.57	.83
2. 1971 black adopters[b]		–	.67	.62	.85
3. Agency outreach			–	.57	.56
4. Sympathetic processing				–	.62
5. Black social workers					–

Source: District of Columbia and Baltimore Adoption Agency Survey.

[a]Correlation coefficients are based on data from 20 agencies. This is a study of a population, not a sample. However, for those accustomed to evaluating coefficients in terms of statistical significance, it may be useful to know that, if this had been a sample, all the coefficients appearing in this table had a probability of less than 1 in 20 of occurring by chance.

[b]Percentage of placements with black adopters.

would encourage black applicants to come to the agency. In terms of agency processing, one might expect the black social worker would be more aware of the economic needs of black families and more understanding, perhaps, of the need for a black adoptive mother to work. A black social worker probably would be more willing to go into a black neighborhood for a home visit, particularly if the visit had to be in the evening.

In addition, one might expect that the black social worker, merely by the fact of her or his existence as an employee of the agency, might make a contribution to agency success in black adoptions. The black applicant coming to the agency might see in that employment hard evidence of the agency's sincerity in its expressed interest in black adopters. Through contacts with the black social worker, the white social workers in the agency might become more understanding of black culture and hence of their black clients. Altogether, it seems quite reasonable that the proportion of agency social workers who are black should be positively correlated with both agency outreach and sympathetic processing. It also seems reasonable that while the percentage of agency placements involving adoptions of blacks by blacks is quite highly correlated with agency outreach and sympathetic processing, the highest correlation would be with the percentage of agency social workers who are black, a variable which seems to combine factors affecting agency outreach, sympathetic processing, and racial understanding.

The information on agency characteristics was collected in 1970. If the activity had begun or the black social worker had been hired shortly before the interviews, it seems reasonable that the impact of that activity or hiring would not have been felt until the next year. In statistical terms, this means that we would expect the correlation coefficients between the key variables and placements with black adopters to increase somewhat between 1970 and 1971. This is exactly what happened. Between 1970 and 1971 the correlation coefficient between agency outreach and the proportion of agency placements which were black increased from .56 to .67. Between sympathetic processing and black placements the increase was from .57 to .62, and between black social workers and black placements the increase was from .83 to .85 (table 2-5).

Table 2-5

Zero- and First-Order Partial Correlations among Key Variables in Study Agencies, Washington, D.C., and Baltimore Agencies, 1970 and 1971[a]

	Adoptions by Blacks	
Key Variables	1970	1971
Agency Outreach[b]	.56	.67
Controlling for[c]		
Number of professionals	.47	.59
Percentage of territory black	.45	.50
Community funding	.53	.64
Favorable social worker attitudes	.38	.53
Sympathetic processing[b]	.57	.62
Controlling for[c]		
Number of professionals	.48	.54
Percentage of territory black	.52	.58
Community funding	.52	.60
Favorable social worker attitudes	.46	.52
Black social workers[b]	.83	.85
Controlling for[c]		
Number of professionals	.77	.80
Percentage of territory black	.79	.81
Community funding	.80	.86
Favorable social worker attitudes	.78	.83

Source: District of Columbia and Baltimore Adoption Agency Survey.

[a]This is a study of a population, not a sample. However, for those accustomed to evaluating coefficients in terms of statistical significance, it may be useful to know that, if this had been a sample, all the zero-order and partial correlation coefficients appearing in this table had a probability of less than 1 in 20 of occurring by chance.

[b]Zero-order correlations.

[c]First-order partial correlations.

The skeptic could ask whether the seemingly close relationship between these factors and black placements is not artificially high, caused by an interaction with one of the variables discussed earlier—agency size, the percentage of agency funds derived from community sources, or the percentage of blacks living in the territory the agency has chosen to serve. By using a statistical device, the first-order partial correlation, it is possible to examine whether this is so.

If the correlation between two factors is fairly high (.60) but that correlation falls to 0 when a third variable is included in the calculation (a first-order partial correlation), this suggests that the third variable is really the important one. Alternatively, if the correlation remains about the same when the third variable is included in the calculation, this suggests that the third variable is not affecting the relationship between the other two. A slight decline in the correlation when the third variable is added suggests that the third variable has some relationship to the other two variables, but not one strong enough to close out the initial observed relationship.

The slight decline is what occurred when we examined the impact of agency size as measured by the number of professionals employed at the agency, agency funding sources (whether the funding was from community sources such as the government or United Givers Funds), the proportion of the population of the agency's territory which was black, and the attitude of agency social workers toward black adopters.

The largest decline between a correlation coefficient and first-order partial correlation occurs when the attitude of the social workers is introduced as a control variable. This suggests that at agencies where social workers are favorable toward black adoptions, the workers introduce outreach and processing procedures which then facilitate placement with black adopters (table 2-5).

Summing Up

Overall, the conclusion to be drawn from this analysis is that the agency interested in black adoptions should hire black social workers, use lots of publicity, and get rid of rules and requirements which exclude many black applicants.

Social workers sometimes say that black families are not interested in adoption. This is true in the sense that blacks are not knocking down agency doors demanding children in the way that white couples sometimes do. However, it is definitely not true in a more meaningful sense. Indeed, it is very clear that, when notified of the availability of children and persuaded that the agency is sincere, black adoptive applicants do come forward in considerable numbers. And when appropriate criteria are used in processing black applicants, considerable numbers of black applicants make it through to adoption.

This chapter described the pressures which were put on the adoption agencies in the District of Columbia and Baltimore in the early 1970s to find more black adoptive homes. With some agencies the pressure worked quite well; at others, less well. A very few did not seem to be affected at all.

One is tempted to speculate that the degree of success attained as a result of the outside pressure was determined in large part by the receptivity of the social workers and policymakers inside the agencies. The presence of black social workers in particular seemed to make a big difference. The importance of black social workers to black adoptions is a continuing theme in the next chapter.

Notes

1. See Dawn Day Wachtel, "Adoption Agencies and the Adoption of Black Children" (Dissertation, University of Michigan, 1972).

2. In all, 272 self-administered questionnaires were completed. For all but three of the agencies, the response rate was 80 percent or higher. The low response rate at the other three agencies was attributable to the social workers' suspicions after the Stern Community Law Firm began advertising for clients to bring lawsuits against adoption agencies. Data collection in terms of the supervisor interviews and administration of the self-administered questionnaires extended from August to December of 1970. Of the 25 agencies originally invited to participate in this study, only one, a suburban county agency, refused.

3. Edmond D. Jones, "On Transracial Adoption of Black Children," *Child Welfare* March 1972, p. 161. Annie Lee Sandusky, Jane Harwood Rea, and Ursula Gallagher, *Families for Black Children* (Washington: Government Printing Office, 1971), pp. 32-33.

4. Carol Honsa, "UGF Refuses to Question Eligibility of Seven Agencies," *Washington Post* May 20, 1970. Martin Weil, "Black Fund Sets Goal of $1 Million," *Washington Post* September 25, 1970. Carl Bernstein, "UGF Vows More Black Aid," *Washington Post* February 14, 1970, p. B-1.

5. Aaron Latham, "Law Firm Offers Aid in Adoption," *Washington Post* September 25, 1970.

6. Around 1969 the two sectarian agencies made a few home studies of black applicants as part of cooperative publicity efforts in their cities which had brought in large numbers of black adoptive applicants. However, the commitment of the agencies was short-term. Supervisors saw this only as a way of helping out other agencies during an overload, not as part of their own agencies' missions. Two or three placements with black adopters were made in this way. In the statistics, the placements are credited to the agencies which took the initiative in attracting the adoptive applicants and who provided the black

children who were adopted—not to the two agencies which did the home studies but did not define themselves as involved with black adopters.

7. T. Bradley, "An Exploration of Caseworkers' Perceptions of Adoptive Applicants," *Child Welfare* October 1966, p. 435.

8. David Fanshel, *A Study of Negro Adoption* (New York: Child Welfare League of America, 1957).

9. For a discussion of the importance of social networks to employment recruitment, see Alfred W. Blumrosen, *Black Employment and the Law* (New Brunswick, N.J.: Rutgers University Press, 1971), p. 229.

10. Otto Kerner, *Report of the National Advisory Commission on Civil Disorders* (New York: Bantam Books, 1968), p. 22.

11. Andrew Billingsley, *Black Families in White America* (Englewood Cliffs, N.J.: Prentice-Hall, 1968), p. 193.

12. Edward O. Laumann, *Bonds of Pluralism: The Form and Substance of Urban Social Networks* (New York: Wiley, 1972).

13. Mildred Hawkins, "Negro Adoptions—Challenge Accepted," *Child Welfare* December 1960, pp. 22-27. Marie W. Daugherty, Hortense W. Few, and Margaret G. Muller, "Achieving Adoption for Sixty Negro Children," *Child Welfare* October 1968, pp. 7-11. Bernice J. Daniels, "Significant Considerations in Placing Negro Infants for Adoption," *Child Welfare* January 1950, p. 11. Phyllis Dunne, "Placing Children of Minority Groups for Adoption," *Children* March-April 1958, pp. 43-48. Walter A. Heath, "Mass Communication Methods in Recruiting Minority Group Adoptive Homes," *Public Welfare* July 1955, pp. 110-114, 134.

14. Eugene Litwak and Henry Meyer, "A Balance Theory of Coordination between Bureaucratic Organizations and Community Primary Groups," *Administrative Science Quarterly* June 1966, pp. 31-58.

15. As reported by an agency supervisor.

16. The neighborhood was defined as black or integrated if 80 percent of the social workers handling adoptive applicants reported that it was.

17. Either the agency supervisor reported these efforts or at least 10 percent of the social workers working with adoptive applicants reported making such efforts themselves. The low (10 percent) breaking point was chosen because contacting leaders within the black community is a task which could easily be delegated to only one or two people.

18. Either the supervisor reported this or at least 30 percent of the social workers working with adoptive applicants reported they themselves had often done this. The dividing line of 30 percent was chosen because through its use the answers given by the supervisors for their own agencies corresponded most closely with the responses of the social workers.

19. Either the agency supervisor or at least 50 percent of the social workers working with adoptive applicants reported doing this often.

20. As reported by an agency supervisor.

21. As reported by an agency supervisor.

22. Clarence D. Fischer, "Homes for Black Children," *Child Welfare* February 1971, p. 110; and Lucille J. Grow and Ann W. Shyne, *Requests for Child Welfare Services* (New York: Child Welfare League of America, 1967), p. 44.

23. Edmond D. Jones, "On Transracial Adoption of Black Children," *Child Welfare* March 1972, p. 158.

24. Daugherty, Few, and Muller, "Achieving Adoption for Sixty Negro Children." Hawkins, "Negro Adoptions—Challenge Accepted." Martha Perry, "An Experiment in Recruitment of Negro Adoptive Parents," *Social Casework* May 1958, p. 295. Heath, "Mass Communication Methods," p. 114. Sister Frances Jerome Wood and Alice C. Lancaster, "Cultural Factors in Negro Adoptive Parenthood," *Social Work* October 1962, pp. 14-21. I.W. Fellner, "Recruiting Adoptive Applicants," *Social Work* January 1968, pp. 92-100.

25. Fischer, "Homes for Black Children," p. 110. Elizabeth Lawder et al., *A Study of Black Adoption Families: A Comparison of a Traditional and a Quasi-Adoption Program* (New York: Child Welfare League of America, 1971), p. 3.

26. Wood and Lancaster, "Cultural Factors in Negro Adoptive Parenthood"; Hawkins, "Negro Adoptions—Challenge Accepted," p. 27; and Fellner, "Recruiting Adoptive Applicants."

27. Fellner, "Recruiting Adoptive Applicants." Raymond Mondloh, "Changing Practice in the Adoptive Home Study," *Child Welfare* March 1969, pp. 148-159. Thomas E. Nutt and John A. Snyder, "Transracial Adoption," report submitted to National Institute of Mental Health, February 1973, pp. 19, 26. Joyce Ladner, *Mixed Families,* (Garden City, N.Y.: Anchor Press/Doubleday, 1977), pp. 57-58. Drucilla Ramey, "Washington's Peculiar Institution" (Paper, Yale University Law School), 1971, p. 65. Elizabeth Herzog et al., *Families for Black Children: The Search for Adoptive Parents* (Washington: Government Printing Office, 1971), p. 45. Daugherty, Few, and Muller, "Achieving Adoption for Sixty Negro Children." Fischer, "Homes for Black Children." Lois Pettit, "Some Observations on the Negro Culture in the United States," *Social Work* July 1960, pp. 104-109. Alfred Kadushin, "Child Welfare," *Research in the Social Services: A Five-Year Review,* ed. Henry S. Maas (New York: National Association of Social Workers, 1966), p. 16.

28. Only those who participated in placement decisions were included in the study and used to define agency size. By this definition, all clerical workers were excluded. In research on industrial organization in England, Woodward also found that the size of the professional staff was a good indicator of agency size. See Joan Woodward, *Industrial Organization: Theory and Practice* (London: Oxford Press, 1965), p. 55.

29. Maurine Beasley, "Blacks Adopt Higher Ratio of Own Race," *Washington Post* April 30, 1973. Betty Medsger, "Parents Cross Racial Lines to Adopt Babies: Asian, Black Infants Sought," *Washington Post* May 30, 1972.

3

Getting Through the System

Judy Fliegenspan

What types of clients do social workers encourage? Discourage? Why do some clients drop out? Why are some clients rejected? What role does race play when the client is black and the social worker is white?

This chapter examines these questions by using the case records of all those who applied to adopt at New York City's Department of Social Services, Division of Adoption Services, in 1972 and had at least one face-to-face interview. The agency had 207 black applicants in 1972 and hired both black and white social workers; thus the agency afforded an ideal opportunity to examine adoption processing in general and the impact on that processing of the race of the social worker in particular.[1]

The year 1972 was chosen because case records were readily available. Staff turnover had been minimal in that year, and sufficient time had elapsed for most applicants to have completed the process and either have adopted or been rejected.

The Agency

The Division of Adoption Services was created primarily to provide services to black families. It was established in 1960 with the aid of a federal grant. At that time, the majority of agencies throughout the New York metropolitan area, including those sponsored by Protestant organizations, were doing little to find homes for black children. Consequently, the number of black children in need of placement was increasing steadily with no appreciable increase in the number of available homes.

In the beginning, the only applicants processed by the division were foster parents who wished to adopt their own foster children. There were no efforts made to recruit beyond this particular group, nor was the agency involved in working directly with biological parents. Reluctance to initiate recruitment drives was based on the belief that black families were not that interested in adopting. Concomitantly, no efforts were made to work with biological parents for the purpose of freeing black children for adoption, for it was feared that no homes would be found for these children.

During the 1960s, the Division of Adoption Services began to expand its program. The number of social workers was increased from 5 to over 20. One

group of social workers handled interstate and intercounty adoptions. Another
provided direct services to natural parents.

In addition to social work staff, the agency also employed a pediatrician,
a psychiatrist, an office manager, and a public relations representative. Recruitment campaigns for adoptive parents were initiated via television, newspapers
and other publications, community groups, businesses, and so on.

The Social Worker

During 1972 the division was operating with 29 social workers, all of whom
were women and 6 of whom were black. New York law requires that workers
doing home studies have a master's degree in social work. All the workers but
one had this degree; the social worker without it only supervised families after
placement and processed some families applying for a second child.

The social workers were hired from a pool of social workers requesting
transfers from other parts of the agency and from among students who did
field placement in adoptions and then requested permanent positions after
completion of course work.

The social workers ranged in age from 26 to 55, with over two-thirds
between the ages of 31 and 40. Over half of the social workers were single.
Two-thirds of those who were married had children; one single and one
divorced worker also had children.

Over three-fourths of the social workers reported they had between three
and nine years' experience in adoption.

The factor which distinguished black and white workers to some extent
was age. Two of the six black workers were under the age of 30; none of the
white workers were that young. The distribution of other characteristics,
such as marital status, parenthood, and experience in adoption, were essentially
the same for both black and white social workers.[2]

The Applicants

In 1972 these social workers had personal interviews with 315 applicants, and
those 315 applicants comprise our study group. The 1850 persons who made
telephone inquiries but had no personal interview were excluded because
records were inadequate.

Of the 315 adoptive applicants, two-thirds were black. The remaining one-
third was almost entirely made up of people from Hispanic and other white
ethnic groups. Less than 3 percent of all applicants were Oriental.

Information on these applicants was gathered from the case records of the
division, and it is from these records that we can garner a picture of the adoptive
applicants.

Some of the applicants were fairly well off. About half had incomes in 1971 of over $15,000 and savings of over $1000. One-fourth owned their own homes, and about two-thirds had space enough so that their adopted child could have a room of her or his own. About 85 percent of all applicants were married couples. Virtually all the husbands and two-thirds of the wives worked. About a third of the applicants had attended college. Some of the people applying to adopt already had children in their homes; most commonly the child was a biological child, although some of the children were adopted, and a few were foster children. About 10 percent of the husbands and 30 percent of the wives had recognized fertility problems.

Of those applicants who were married, almost half had been married over seven years. For 85 percent of the couples, this was their first marriage; for 85 percent also, both partners were of the same religion. For about 40 percent of the couples, both the husband and wife were under 30.

On many characteristics, black and white applicants were quite similar. However, black couples had less savings and were less likely to have a separate room available for their new child. Black husbands were less likely to be working in white-collar jobs than their white counterparts. Black applicants had less higher education than white applicants. As a group, black applicants were a little older and, in husband-and-wife households, somewhat more likely to share the same religion. Single persons represented a quarter of all black applicants and only 3 percent of white applicants (table 3-1).

The Successful Applicants

Not all those who wanted to adopt were ultimately able to do so. Of the 315 couples and individuals who applied to adopt in 1972, a quarter were finally approved. The approval rate for black applicants was 23 percent; for white applicants, 30 percent.

The approved group included families that had completed adoption through the courts, families that had received a child but not yet completed adoption, and a few families that had been approved but were still waiting for a child at the time data were collected. The nonapproved group was made up of all applicants who were not approved for placement or who dropped out before a child was placed in their home. It also included a very small number of applicants who received a child that was later returned to or removed by the agency and who were not given another child.

In approving applicants for adoption, social workers seem to have been influenced by certain characteristics. For example, approval rates were higher for married people than for singles; higher for people who owned their own homes than for people who did not; higher for people who had a room set aside for their expected child compared to people who did not; and higher for couples where the wife was not working than for couples where she was working (table 3-2).

Table 3-1
**Percentage of Adoptive Applicants with Selected Characteristics, by Race,
New York City Division of Adoption Services, 1972**

	Applicants[a]		
Applicant Characteristics	Black (n = 207)	White[b] (n = 108)	Total% (n = 315)
Economic security			
Income over $15,000	45	43	45
Savings over $1,000	51	65	57
Own home	27	26	27
Own room for child	63	69	65
Employment status			
Husband employed	96	97	97
and white-collar	42	55	49
Wife employed	70	51	64
and white-collar	56	48	52
Education			
Husband beyond high school	26	47	35
Wife beyond high school	35	44	38
Children and fertility			
Have biological child	23	23	23
Have adopted child	10	9	10
Have foster child	3	6	4
Husband fertility problem	9	12	10
Wife fertility problem	33	26	30
Marital status			
Single	25	3	17
Married	75	97	84
Married over 7 years	45	41	44
First marriage for both	84	91	87
Other			
Husband and wife same religion	90	80	86
Husband and wife both under 30	38	48	41
Total	100	100	100

Source: New York City Division of Adoption Services case study.

[a]These figures represent the maximum number of cases. Totals vary for different characteristics because, for some applicants, information on some characteristics was not collected before they either were rejected or dropped out. Percentages are calculated on the number of applicants for whom a particular characteristic was reported.

[b]In this and subsequent tables in this chapter, the term "white applicants" refers to all nonblack applicants to the division. In 1972 there were 108 nonblack applicants; 30 were Hispanic and 3 were couples including at least one Oriental partner.

Given the seeming preference for people who are conventional and well off, the lower acceptance rate for husbands in white-collar occupations seems surprising. But on closer examination, approval rates on occupation fit the pattern

Table 3-2
Percentage of Applicants Approved, by Selected Characteristics and Race of Applicants, New York City Division of Adoption Services, 1972

	Applicants		
Applicant Characteristics	Black	White	Total
All applicants	23	30	25
Home ownership			
Owned	46	48	47
Not owned	16	25	19
Own room for child			
Yes	37	44	40
No	23	23	23
Income			
Over $15,000	43	30	39
$15,000 and under	26	45	33
Husband's occupation			
White-collar	27	32	30
Not white-collar	33	33	33
Employment status of wife			
Employed	19	19	19
Not employed	36	43	39
Marital status			
Married	29	30	30
Single	4	0	3
Years married			
Over 7	33	35	34
7 or less	27	27	27
Age			
One or both partners over 30	28	34	30
Both partners under 30	17	25	20
Education of husband			
Beyond high school	36	34	35
High school or less	37	38	37
Education of wife			
Beyond high school	26	32	29
High school or less	34	42	37

Source: New York City Division of Adoption Services case study.

also. The approved blue-collar husbands were in the higher-paying occupations; they were truck drivers, machinists, and skilled laborers. The white-collar husbands who were not approved were apt to hold lower-paid jobs; they were bank tellers, clerical workers, and semiprofessionals.

The higher acceptance rates for wives of lower educational levels may be related to a tendency of less educated wives to be willing to stop work after the arrival of the adopted child. The different acceptance rates for different groups seems counter to the agency's own published guidelines, which stated that applicants were to be selected on the basis of the division's estimate of their capacity and potential as adoptive parents for available children and not on the basis of certain characteristics of the applicant.[3] At the time this study was done, New York State had an adoption subsidy which was available to families with low incomes.

Why People Do Not Adopt

Very few people were actually turned down as adoptive applicants. Most of those who were not approved for placement simply withdrew somewhere along the way. Why did they withdraw? The case records suggest a variety of answers: financial difficulties, change in health, unavailability of a child, psychological unreadiness, and failure to maintain contact with the agency.

Failure to maintain contact with the agency was a catch-all category. Undoubtedly it included some people who had changed their minds about adoption, but probably it also included people who were discouraged by some real or imagined obstacle to their completing adoption. The category "failure to maintain contact" implies a failure in communication between social worker and client. If good rapport had been established, the client would have told the worker why he or she was withdrawing. Almost 40 percent of the black clients withdrew without giving a reason. Less than 20 percent of the white clients did so (table 3-3).

The Process

In order to better understand what happened to black applicants, it is helpful to examine the adoption process, beginning with the time the applicant first approaches the agency.

The entire processing period, from the point of initial inquiry until the child was placed in the home, can be divided into four distinct stages:

I.   Initial inquiry to setting up of the first interview
II. First interview and completion of the application to adopt
III. Home study and approval for placement
IV. Placement of the child

During each stage, workers had some leeway, but before applicants could move from one stage to the next, workers had to get the supervisor's approval.

Table 3-3
Reason for Termination of Contact, by Race of Applicant, New York City Division of Adoption Services, 1972
(percentage)

Reason	White Applicants *(n = 76)*	Black Applicants		
		Total (n = 159)	*Black Workers (n = 32)*	*White[a] Workers (n = 127)*
Failure to maintain contact with agency	17	38	28	41
Psychological unreadiness	8	24	22	24
Other reasons[b]	75	38	50	35
Financial difficulties	7	12	9	13
Change in health	8	12	16	11
Unavailability of child	38	7	9	6
Pregnancy	12	2	6	1
Moved	7	0	0	0
Other	3	5	9	4
Total	100	100	100	100

Source: New York City Division of Adoption Services case study.

[a]White is used to refer to all nonblack social workers, including one Oriental woman.

[b]May not add, since some applicants had more than one reason for termination.

Stage I

In 1972 the initial inquiry, usually a phone call, was answered by a receptionist or clerk who recorded the applicant's name, address, telephone number, race, marital status, family size, and type of child requested. This information was then forwarded to the director, who in turn gave the inquiry to either of two higher-ranking supervisors. The higher-ranking supervisor would decide which of the units was next in line for a case and pass it on. The unit supervisor would then assign the case to a particular social worker. The basis for the assignment of cases to particular workers varied. It was not agency policy to assign cases on the basis of race. However, in 1972 black social workers did have a somewhat higher proportion of black clients in their caseloads than white social workers did—76 percent compared with 63 percent.

Once an applicant was assigned to a worker, the applicant usually remained with that worker until termination of contact. Apart from normal occurrences such as resignations, illnesses, and promotions, applicants were rarely transferred from one worker to another. About 15 percent of the applicants in 1972 experienced a shift to a second social worker. Two families were seen by three workers each. When more than one social worker worked with a client, the last worker to have contact with the client was the one to whom the outcome, approval or disapproval, was assigned.[4]

Having received the assignment, the social worker contacted the client to introduce herself and arrange for a first interview. In the case of married couples, agency regulations required that the first interview include both husband and wife.

For some applicants, another part of this stage was an introductory group meeting. The agency initiated group meetings in mid-1972 to prepare applicants for the home study and to inform them of the kinds of children available. Since few white children were available for adoption, the real purpose of the meeting probably was to discourage white applicants. This is reflected in the fact that only 15 percent of the black applicants compared with 25 percent of white applicants ever attended the introductory group meetings.

The original intention had been to schedule the group meetings on a weekly basis. In fact, they were held less frequently. For those directed to the group meetings, the meetings occurred before the applicants were assigned to a particular worker. With black applicants, usually it took three contacts, by mail or phone or both, spread out over six to nine weeks before the first meeting with the social worker was arranged. Stage I ended just before the first meeting between the social worker and the applicant took place (table 3-4).

Stage II

The second stage of the process included the first face-to-face interview between the social worker and the clients and preparation to initiate the home study. The purpose of the first interview was to get acquainted. Generally the worker described the adoption procedure, informed the applicants of the kinds of children available, and noted both the type of child requested and the applicants' reason for seeking adoption. She gathered some background data.

At her discretion, the worker could encourage the clients by presenting the positive aspects of adoption and by indicating that she would help with any problems that might arise. The worker also could discourage the clients by giving misleading information about the kinds of children available, by giving hints of rigid requirements, or by appearing judgmental.

At the conclusion of the interview, the worker gave out an application form, to be filled out at home and returned to the agency. In some instances, a worker would request to see a document before an application could be considered complete. Occasionally, a worker would assist a client with an application if she felt the family might have difficulty completing the form on their own.

Table 3-4
Black Clients: Type and Number of Contacts and Mean Weeks in Stage, by Race of Worker and whether Client Adopted, New York City Division of Adoption Services, 1972

Type and Number of Contacts	All Workers		Black Workers		White Workers	
	Client Adopted	Client Did Not Adopt	Client Adopted	Client Did Not Adopt	Client Adopted	Client Did Not Adopt
Stage I	9	6	10	6	7	6
Stage II	4	4	5	5	3	4
Stage III	30	25	39	29	21	20
Stage IV[a]	26	34	29	28	24	39
Mean weeks in stage, all stages	69	68	83	68	55	69
Stage I	3	3	3	3	3	3
Stage II	2	2	2	2	1	2
Stage III	8	5	9	5	7	5
Stage IV[a]	4	7	3	3	5	9
Average number of contacts, all stages	16	16	17	12	16	18
Stage I	b	b	b	b	b	b
Stage II	1	1	1	1	1	1
Stage III	3	2	3	2	3	2
Stage IV[a]	1	1	1	1	1	1
Average number of face-to-face contacts, all stages	5	4	5	3	5	4

Source: New York City Division of Adoption Services case study.

Note: Some columns may not add due to rounding.

[a]Applicants approved to adopt their own foster child were excluded from the analysis at this stage, since the child was already in the home.

[b]Less than 0.5 percent.

Unfortunately, some workers linked good parenthood with the ability to comply with bureaucratic procedures. Therefore, for these workers, completing the application and returning it as quickly as possible was viewed as the client's responsibility and taken as motivation to continue in the process. If an application was not returned within a "sufficient period of time," some workers would close a case, while others would contact the client to ask if further assistance was needed.

The home study was usually initiated after receipt of the completed application form, although this could vary.

The second stage usually took eight or nine weeks and involved an average of one contact between the social worker and the applicants in addition to the personal interview.

Stage III

The third stage was the home study. It consisted of a home visit and office interviews. The applicants had to provide such things as medical reports, fertility reports, reference letters, marriage certificate, bank statements, pay stubs, and any other evaluative information which the worker deemed necessary. The worker herself could decide which documents were needed.

Workers could be flexible in terms of the number of interviews required, although generally there were three. During the interviews applicants were asked to provide personal information about themselves, both current and past. The social worker would make inquiries about living arrangements (would the child have a room of its own?), child care plans if the mother would be working, child rearing and disciplinary practices, and so on.

For those black applicants who were successful, this stage ended when they were approved for placement of a child. The 30 weeks it took to complete the stage was almost double the 16 weeks an agency brochure promised as typical.[5]

Stage IV

Stage IV was the period in which the applicant awaited placement of a child. Generally the worker would select a child which she felt was suitable for the family and describe the child to them. If they were interested, the worker would arrange a time and place for "showing" the child. The applicants had the option of rejecting a child prior to the showing or after the showing. The worker, too, could veto a placement by deciding, on whatever basis, that the child was not really suitable for the family.

In a few instances, if the child was beyond infancy, the family and child would meet a number of times before the child was actually placed in the home. This was done to ease the trauma of separation from the foster home for the child and to give the family and child time to get to know one another. When the applicants and worker felt ready, the child was officially placed in the home, and the period of supervision after placement began.

Successful black applicants had an average of four contacts, usually one in person, with their social worker during this stage. The contacts extended over half a year. At the time data were collected for this study, three black families

had not yet received a child. Since there were so many black children available
for adoption, it is surprising that black families had to wait so long.

All told, in 1972 the successful black applicants to the Division of Adoption
Services spent close to a year and a half in the adoption process. In that period
they were in touch with their social workers a little less than once a month.
They had five personal interviews and had contact an additional ten or eleven
times by phone and letter.

Of those black applicants who were not successful, some dropped out at
every stage. About 1200 blacks called in to inquire about adoption during 1972;
207 had the first interview; a home study was begun on 113; 58 were approved
for adoption; 42 finally ended up with a child; and an additional 3 black applicants were approved and still waiting for a child to be placed with them when
data collection for this study ended.[6]

It seems likely that both the black workers and the white workers could
have eliminated some of the dropouts if the agency's policies had been more
flexible—if the first interviews with clients occurred within a week or two of the
first contact instead of after six to nine weeks and if the first interview could
have been at the applicant's home, if that is what the applicant preferred, and
so on. The great value of flexible and appropriate processing is explored more
in chapter 7. The opportunity here is to trace the impact of the race of the
social worker on the applicant dropout rate, by using the workers' own case
records.

The Case Records

Almost no records were kept of callers who were lost before the first interview.
However, once a social worker met with the applicants, it is possible to follow
the applicants' paths in considerable detail.

In theory, the case records contain accounts of all phone calls, letters, and
personal interviews between social workers and clients.[7] And, in fact, the
records did contain quite a bit of detail. Social workers were particularly careful to record the client's movement or failure to move from one stage to the
next. We will always wonder what was missing from the records, of course; but
given the present detail, we are confident that we know much of what happened.

Probably there is a slant to the case material, but it is the social worker's
own view; and since we are particularly interested in what the social worker was
doing and thinking, having her slant is an advantage.

Case records were examined to establish the number of contacts between
social workers and applicants; whether the contacts were face to face, phone, or
letter; and the number of weeks applicants spent in each stage. The character
of the contact between the workers and their clients was also studied.

It had been anticipated that clients would feel better treated and be less

likely to drop out during the application process if their applications were
speedily processed (this assumes that slow movement is interpreted as a form
of rejection), if they had relatively more contact with the social worker (this
assumes that more contact means easier communication), and if they felt the
social worker was favorably disposed toward them.

Of these three, only the last expectation was fulfilled. There seemed to be
no consistent pattern between the number of contacts with the social worker
and whether the client dropped out. Also, there was no obvious relationship
between the length of time the client spent in particular stages and whether the
client made it through to adoption (table 3-4).[8]

Encouraging Clients

There were a variety of ways that a social worker could encourage or discourage
a client. Two general categories—facilitative and nonfacilitative—were used.
Comments defined as nonfacilitative included

> Any attempt by the worker to discourage the client about the kinds of
> children available. (With so many black children available for adoption,
> the supply of children should not have been an issue.)

> Any attempt by the worker to act contrary to the official literature with
> respect to applicant qualifications, such as requiring that the applicants sub-
> mit to expensive fertility tests (which can be psychologically and physically
> painful), requiring documents that were not readily available, and delays
> in the process due to the above.

> Any indication of a judgmental attitude regarding the couples' family back-
> ground.

Nonfacilitative contacts were useful to social workers in encouraging clients to
drop out. It was much easier for a social worker to have someone withdraw
than to have to say "you are rejected." In some instances the delays and discouragement were more subtle than at other times. Below are examples of
facilitative and nonfacilitative comments.

The application

Nonfacilitative: The worker states that completion of the application "will indicate to us that you wish to continue."

Facilitative: The family is encouraged to ask questions about the application
blank, and the worker further suggests that the family phone if they have other
questions and need assistance.

Other forms

Nonfacilitative: Although the application form has been completed, the worker says that the home study cannot begin until all the family members' medical forms are completed and returned.

Facilitative: The worker sets up an appointment for the first home visit and suggests that the family members have their medical reports done and sent to her upon completion.

Risks and rewards of adoption

Nonfacilitative: The worker mentions that the applicants are probably well aware of the problems associated with adopted children and then proceeds to point out all the genetic, psychological, and emotional problems that can arise.

Facilitative: The worker notes that raising an adopted child may be different in some ways (but just as rewarding) as raising a biological child. She points to the positive aspects of adoption and reassures the clients that the agency will help them prepare for their new family member.

Working mothers

Nonfacilitative: The social worker indicates that if the home is approved, the agency will expect the mother to stay home with the child for a least a few months after placement.

Facilitative: The worker discusses the feasibility of the wife taking some time off from her job after the child is placed and also discusses alternative plans for child care.

Employment record

Nonfacilitative: The worker indicates she has spoken with one of the husband's previous employers and in one instance termination occurred as a result of an argument.

Facilitative: The worker acknowledges that the husband's employment changes have improved his position.

Missed meetings

Nonfacilitative: A note from the worker states, "Since I have not heard from you, I assume that you have decided against adoption at this time. However, if you still wish to discuss the matter, you can telephone."

Facilitative: A note from the worker states, "You missed the appointment scheduled for _____ ; I attempted to telephone the morning of_____ , but received no answer. Perhaps we misunderstood each other about the time or the date, or perhaps something is troubling you which you hesitate to discuss. Please telephone as soon as possible."

Each personal interview and each mail or phone contact between the social worker and client which the worker initiated was given an overall rating as either facilitative or nonfacilitative.[9] Client-initiated contacts through mail or phone were not so categorized because the character of the social worker's response was difficult to assess. Sometimes, as in the case of a letter from the client, there was no response at all.

In order to assess whether facilitative contacts made any difference, the black clients of the social workers were divided into two groups: those who finally adopted and those who did not. Some 77 percent of the contacts of those who finally adopted were facilitative; 64 percent of the contacts of those who did not adopt were facilitative. The proportion of contacts which were facilitative varied in the different stages. In the first stage, before the social worker and client had met, almost all the contacts for all the clients were facilitative (table 3-5).

In the second stage, where worker and clients first met and where the client was asked to complete the application form, sharp differences arose. Those applicants who ultimately adopted enjoyed many more facilitative contacts during this phase than those who terminated. The facilitative contacts probably helped the clients deal with their uncertainties and insecurities. Pursuit by the

Table 3-5
Black Clients: Percentage of Contacts which Were Facilitative, by Stage, Race of Worker, and whether Client Adopted, New York City Division of Adoption Services, 1972

	All Workers		Black Workers		White Workers	
Stage	Client Adopted	Client Did Not Adopt	Client Adopted	Client Did Not Adopt	Client Adopted	Client Did Not Adopt
Stage I	87	86	83	85	89	86
Stage II	85	47	74	57	91	45
Stage III	76	60	70	67	79	57
Stage IV[a]	69	58	72	83	68	54
All stages	77	64	72	70	79	62

Source: New York City Division of Adoption Services case study.

[a]Applicants approved to adopt their own foster child were excluded from the analysis at this stage, since the child was already in the home.

social workers also helped bring some applicants back into the process who otherwise would have been discouraged by a misunderstanding of the requirements for adoptive parenthood or intimidated about filling out the form.

During the home study and placement stages, clients who adopted received more facilitative contacts than those who did not. It is easy to see how a positive attitude on the part of the social workers would encourage applicants and help them deal with both the frustration of waiting and the anxieties which all adoptive applicants must feel.

Facilitative Contacts and Race of the Worker

The relationship between facilitative contacts and whether the client ultimately adopted changes when the clients of white workers are separated from those of black workers. In stage I, black workers and white workers treated their black clients about the same. However, in stages II through IV, the workers treated their clients differently. The white workers consistently had many more facilitative contacts with their completing clients compared to those who dropped out. The black workers, on the other hand, had a much more varied pattern. At no time was the gap between favored and less favored clients of black workers as large as that for white workers. And, in fact, in stage III black workers gave both groups about the same proportion of positive contacts. In stage IV, black workers gave a greater proportion of facilitative contacts to clients who dropped out than to clients who adopted.

In general, compared to white workers, the black workers tried harder with clients who were dropping out and less hard with clients who ultimately adopted. It is as if the white social workers had a two-track system: in order to compensate for problems of communication across racial lines, those clients who were perceived favorably were given special treatment; those clients who were perceived unfavorably were given nonfacilitative treatment and encouraged to drop out as quickly as possible. The special treatment worked. When white social workers showered their black clients with facilitative contacts, the clients did adopt.

Favored Clients

Both the black social workers and the white social workers tended to favor black clients who were well off, married, in their thirties, and where the wife did not plan to work (table 3-6). But there the similarity ends.

In every case, the acceptance rates of black workers were higher than those of white workers. For example, black applicants who had a separate room set aside for their new child had an overall acceptance rate of 42 percent with black

Table 3-6
Percentage of Black Applicants Approved, by Selected Applicant Characteristics and Race of Social Worker, New York City Division of Adoption Services, 1972

	Black Applicants	
Applicant Characteristics	*Black Worker*	*White Worker*
All applicants	32	21
Home ownership		
Owned	50	48
Not owned	23	14
Own room for child		
Yes	42	36
No	29	21
Income		
Over $15,000	53	39
$15,000 and under	26	25
Husband blue-collar[a]	50	27
Employment Status of wife		
Employed	23	18
Not employed	50	30
Married[a]	42	26
Married		
Over 7 years	56	25
7 years or less	29	27
Age		
One or both partners over 30	42	24
Both partners under 30	19	16
Education high school or less[a]		
Wife	44	30
Husband	48	32

Source: New York City Division of Adoption Services case study.

[a]Sufficient data were not available to report acceptance rates for white-collar husbands, singles, and college-educated people.

workers and only 36 percent with white workers. Black applicants whose newly adopted child would have to share a room had an acceptance rate of 29 percent with black workers and only 21 percent with white workers. Working wives had an acceptance rate of 23 percent with black workers and 18 percent with white workers. Wives who were full-time homemakers had an acceptance rate of 50 percent with black workers and only 30 percent with white workers. Overall, black clients with black workers had an acceptance rate of 32 percent; black clients with white workers had an acceptance rate of only 21 percent.

Black Workers Do Better

Not only did white workers have proportionately more clients who dropped out; but also among those who dropped out, there was a strong indication of a problem in the casework relationship. Over 40 percent of the black clients of white workers left without even telling their workers why they were dropping out (not maintaining contact). Less than 30 percent of the black clients of black workers left without an explanation (table 3-3).

The differences between black workers and white workers relate to differences between groups of workers as a whole and are not the result of the extraordinary activity of one or two individuals. As can be seen from table 3-7, 5 of the 6 black social workers exhibited above-average approval rates. Only 6 of the 23 white workers had approval rates above average.

It is also noteworthy that none of the other characteristics of social workers—

Table 3-7

Percentage of Social Workers with High and Low Approval Rates, by Selected Characteristics of Workers, New York City Division of Adoption Services, 1972

Worker Characteristics	Number of Workers	Total	High Approval Rates[a]	Low Approval Rates[a]
Race				
Black	6	100	83	17
White	23	100	26	74
Age				
Under 36 years	16	100	37	63
36 years and over	10	100	50	50
Marital status				
Single	14	100	36	64
Married	9	100	56	44
Divorced	3	100	33	67
Parenthood				
Child or children	8	100	50	50
No children	18	100	39	61
Experience in adoption				
Under 5 years	14	100	36	64
5 years and over	12	100	50	50

Source: New York City Division of Adoption Services case study.

[a]High approval rates refer to rates above the mean approval rate (27 percent for clients of all races). Low rates refer to those rates below the mean.

age, marital status, parenthood, experience in adoption—showed as strong a
relationship to high approval rates as being black.

Because of the great need for black adopters, the focus has been on problems which arise when white social workers interact with black clients. But it is
of interest to explore the other interracial pair as well: the black worker and
the white client. Here there are few cases to examine, but those few cases suggest that there is no problem. Black workers appear to relate as well to white
applicants as to black applicants. The approval rates are virtually the same
(table 3-8).

In her graduate education and employment, the black social worker was
probably surrounded by whites. She had to learn to understand whites in order
to get along. The white worker, also surrounded by whites in graduate work
and employment, has not had to learn about blacks.

The average white client has probably not experienced racial discrimination
from a black person in a position of authority. The average black client undoubtedly has experienced racial discrimination from whites in positions of
authority. The racial pairs seem to be mirror images of each other, but in social
reality they are not.

The justification for utilizing black professionals often has been based on an
expressed need in the black community. However, the evidence in this chapter
suggests that black workers are just as capable of working with white clients as
white workers are. Yet black professionals are not often hired to serve white
clients.

The data also suggest that white workers have difficulty working with black
clients; ironically, white workers are often hired to serve black clients. The
possible sources of the white worker-black client problems are considered in
chapters 4 and 5.

Table 3-8
**Applicants Approved, by Race of Applicant and Race of Social Worker, New
York City Division of Adoption Services, 1972**

| | Black Workers | | | White Workers | | |
	Total Applicants	Number Approved	Percentage of Total	Total Applicants	Number Approved	Percentage of Total
Black applicants	47	15	32	160	34	21
White applicants	15	5	33	93	27	29

Source: New York City Division of Adoption Services case study.

Notes

1. Judy Fliegenspan, "Processing Black Families for Adoption" (Master's thesis, Brooklyn College, 1976).
2. The descriptions are based on information on 23 of the 26 nonblack social workers and all 6 of the black social workers who were employed in the division in 1972. The nonblack social workers included one Oriental worker and one worker of Hispanic origin.
3. Department of Social Services, Bureau of Child Welfare, Division of Adoption Services, "Adoption Guide for Adoptive Applicants and Foster Parents," October 1971.
4. Those applicants who had more than one worker were in the process longer and in most cases eventually were approved.
5. Department of Social Services, "Adoption Guide."
6. There were two black applicants for every white applicant at the time of the initial interview. If this same ratio applied to the 1850 people of all races who called to inquire about adoption, then about 1200 of the callers were black.
7. All evidence of mailed correspondence, completed phone calls, and in-person interviews was analyzed. If a client or worker phoned and there was no answer, this did not count as a contact. If the client stated a letter was never received and there was no copy of the letter in the case record, the social worker's claim that a letter was sent was not counted as a contact. For a detailed discussion of the advantages and disadvantages of utilizing case records as a data source, see Matilda White Riley, "Sociological Research," *A Case Approach*, vol. I (New York: Harcourt, Brace, 1963). Bernard Berelson, *Content Analysis in Communication Research* (Glencoe, Ill.: Free Press, 1952). Robert G. Angell and Ronald Freeman, "The Use of Documents, Records, Census Materials, and Indices," and Dorwin P. Cartwright, "Analyses of Qualitative Material," both in *Research Methods in the Behavioral Sciences*, eds. Leon Festinger and Daniel Katz (New York: Dryden Press, 1953), pp. 300-326, 421-470. Kuno E. Beller, *Clinical Process* (New York: Free Press, 1962).
8. Time was measured in weeks and was calculated from the point the client entered the process stage until the worker noted in the case record that the stage was completed. For applicants who were terminated prior to completing the process, the time interval was calculated to include the last contact between the applicant and the worker, prior to official termination (the actual closing of the case).
9. The final coding schedule was tested for reliability. Two people coded ten case records separately. The differences were discussed, and decisions were made as to how certain information should be coded. Five additional cases were coded separately, and no discrepancy between the two coders was found. The two coders consulted each other whenever a case seemed ambiguous. The

second coder did not know the objectives of the research; and when problems arose regarding the interpretation, the second coder's interpretation was accepted. Finally, the second coder checked entire cases of the other coder. The coding of case records was completed in four months.

White Social Workers and Black Clients

Researchers in social work, counseling, psychotherapy, and education have all found evidence that lack of rapport and negative outcomes are problems in counseling situations involving white workers and black clients.[1] Some of the problems stem from white difficulties in understanding black culture.

Black Culture

Just as an Italian-American subculture, an Eastern European Jewish-American subculture, and a Chinese-American subculture exist, so also does a black American subculture exist. It is this culture which created jazz and the blues. Its current outer manifestations include the Afro haircut, the dashiki, and certain foods. Some black foods have been taken over by the wider society. Others, like hog maws, collard greens, and chitterlings, have not. The basic language is English, but it is English with a difference—a different accent, a different grammar, and a different vocabulary.[2] Black culture includes storefront churches, single-parent families, child-rearing responsibilities for grandparents, working mothers, and differences in style and life situation which are difficult to capture on paper.

Language differences and differences in styles of communication are key. When white workers lack knowledge of language patterns in the black community, they may completely misinterpret feelings that black clients express. The client may say one thing, and the worker may misunderstand and think something entirely different has been said.[3]

For a number of black families, the storefront church with its fervent expressive style is the center of their religious and social life. Spending a great deal of time together at church gives family members many benefits, including increased family cohesion. The storefront church probably offers a warmer, more accepting, new community for an adopted child than the homogeneous, competitive suburbs where people who belong to more conventional churches often live. Unfortunately, white workers, put off by religious behavior they do not understand, sometimes discourage good potential black adopters simply because they are active in nontraditional churches.[4]

Religious orientation affects the attitudes of some black applicants toward infertility. They have not produced a child, and so they conclude that "God did not intend for me to bear a child." Fertility testing seems irrelevant to them. Their lack of interest in this expensive and often inconclusive process is evidence not of a *denial* of infertility but rather of an *acceptance* of it.

In the black community, grandparents and other older relatives sometimes end up raising young children while both parents work. This often works out very well. Thus social workers should not be surprised if middle-aged and older blacks without such responsibilities from their already-existing families are interested in adopting young children. Adoption advertising geared only to young adults misses an important group of potential adopters.[5]

Single-parent families are more common among blacks than among whites, and, contrary to popular stereotypes, many do very well. Thus it is quite appropriate and in keeping with a part of black experience for single persons to adopt.[6]

Two working parents are not uncommon in the black community, and often both incomes are needed to maintain an adequate standard of living. The appropriate question is not whether the wife or husband is willing to quit work, but whether the child care plan is adequate.

Shared Problems

Living in a society which discriminates against them has given black people certain common problems. Thus, for example, a number of black clients, particularly those raised in the South, may have difficulty getting birth certificates or death or divorce certificates.

Many blacks have had to change jobs frequently and to take positions in unrelated fields of employment just to keep a job. Such job instability is evidence of the low social value place on black workers and not evidence of the black workers' personal instability.[7] Job discrimination has kept black incomes down, too, forcing many to live on incomes lower than those enjoyed by many white families. Consequently, the important consideration for adoption workers is not the size of family income, but the family's ability to manage on whatever income there is.[8]

Arrest records should not automatically disqualify black applicants either. As the Black Child Development Institute Task Force has pointed out,

> Arrest records for Blacks are often more of an indication of what a family or individual has survived or overcome rather than an indication of where they are headed. Witness the nation of Islam. Though many of its members have been recruited and converted in prisons and from a variety of "street" activities, they constitute a strong and stable element in Black community life.[9]

Fear and Prejudice

At some point, lack of understanding shades into fear and prejudice.[10] Some white social workers have been reported to be afraid of blacks who wear Afro haircuts, others to be uneasy with Black Muslims and just ordinary black people.[11]

To deal with their prejudices, all whites raised in American society have to come to terms with the general racial stereotypes which are part of American culture. Black and white are more than descriptive terms. They are emotionally laden symbols. God is associated with goodness and light; black, with the devil. We say "pure as the driven snow" and describe a cruel person as "black-hearted." Racial stereotypes include the notion that blacks have less ambition and looser morals than whites and are less concerned about their families.[12] The white social worker who accepts these stereotypes, either consciously or unconsciously, is not able to react appropriately to black clients.

In adoptions, skin color preference is one area where white stereotypes have been a problem. Some white social workers have expressed bewilderment and amusement because some black adopters want children of a particular skin tone while others do not have a preference. What these white workers fail to realize is that the variety in black preferences is similar to the variety in white preferences where some couples want a child very similar to themselves in ethnic background and others do not care.[13]

Workers' attitudes toward skin color impinge inappropriately on the adoption process in other ways also. For example, some workers find light-skinned black children more attractive and attempt to place the light-skinned children, no matter what the adopting families' preferences are.[14]

The white social worker may have strong negative feelings about being close to black people, perhaps surrounded by them. These feelings can come up easily during the home visit, since many black applicants live in all-black neighborhoods. The social workers, uncomfortable at this prospect, especially if the visit has to be made at night, may very well be tempted to get rid of the problem by encouraging the black applicant to drop out before the home visit becomes necessary.

Once blacks internalized their anger about discrimination or identified with the whites (a phenomenon observed with other oppressed groups also). Some blacks are now turning their anger about discrimination against whites, which is a healthy development, especially when the anger is turned toward social change as well. The white social worker needs to be able to see black anger in this light and not be frightened off at the prospect of the person passing on similar attitudes to an adopted child.[15]

The white social workers' feelings about discrimination are also relevant.

To work well with black clients, white social workers must be able to accept the ugliness of racism without denying it or being overwhelmed by guilt.[16]

A lack of concern for blacks sometimes shows itself in the language of equality. At some agencies black applicants have been given preference in processing. Sometimes white workers have complained that this is unfair.[17] Yet if an agency has a backlog of approved white applicants and an oversupply of black children awaiting adoption, giving preference to black applicants is the rational choice. With enough black applicants, the agency may even reach the point where the black children in its custody have the same opportunity to be adopted as the white children.

Social Class and Race

When working with a black working-class applicant, the white social worker has an even wider social gap to span. She has to be very careful not to lose good applicants. By using the definition of a Michigan agency, Spaulding for Children, families can be defined as *working-class*

> . . . if they work at unskilled or semi-skilled employment for an hourly wage, have a junior high school or high school education, do not rely heavily on social acceptance by peers or the community as a measure of family success, and are relaxed about the child's social and educational achievement.[18]

A working-class family can have values different from a middle-class worker. Many working-class families believe

> that sons should behave one way and daughters another;

> that children should promptly obey their parents, regardless of the child's desires;

> that physical punishment is right and necessary;

> that it is all right if their child is not interested in going to college (they may not be able to afford to send the child anyway);

> that they can "get by" on an income a middle-class social worker would find hopelessly inadequate;

> that educated people should be deferred to, even if the working-class person does not agree with what is said (thus a worker should not interpret negatively a family's reluctance to assert their ideas or infer from their silence that they are "passive-aggressive" individuals).

> Working-class speech tends to be descriptive and action-oriented, and

concepts are expressed as analogies or anecdotes. Middle-class persons, unaccustomed to this style of speech, can miss the point. For their part, working-class families can have difficulty understanding workers who talk at length and in abstractions.[19] Black clients, aware of these communication differences, are particularly insecure with white workers.

> There is more fear of rejection among blacks—they feel they have to prove themselves more. They fear they won't be able to express themselves well in the interview. This is said to be especially true of the "lower class." They want to be "more than prepared" in what they see as "a white situation."[20]

One client summed up her feelings about the communication problems this way:

> For some reason I don't like the idea of sitting across the table like you're on the witness stand. It's like judge and jury. When you sit at the desk and they say "Tell me something about yourself and why you want to adopt a child," you feel doomed before you start.[21]

Middle-class social workers can work effectively with working-class clients by changing their approach:

> By being warm and informal in their language and dress and in their attitudes toward themselves and their clients

> By talking in a straightforward and easily understood manner

> By clarifying procedures and explaining the reasons for delays, even when not specifically asked to do so

> By accepting values different from their own

> By dealing with their own discomfort at having clients who are not accustomed to extensive verbal expression of ideas, beliefs, and attitudes.[22]

Appointments, Time, and the Working Class

Working-class clients often feel powerless relative to middle-class adoption workers. This feeling of powerlessness affects the working-class client's approach to making appointments. Rather than protest an appointment that is inappropriate in time or place, the working-class client is likely to agree to attend and then decide not to go. Also, the working-class client, given an appointment, may not understand that the social worker really means to have the meeting at that particular time. The working-class clients' other experiences have probably been

with agencies where the clients were kept waiting no matter when they arrived
and where appointments were given out without regard to the client's other
commitments. Such a case is that of a woman who was always two hours late
for her child's clinic appointment. She had to be home at two o'clock to
meet her other children at the school bus. Nonetheless, she was continually
given two o'clock appointments at the clinic.[23]

Aware of the potential for problems of this sort, the social worker certainly should not use punctuality as a test of interest in adoption. Nor should
a worker assume that a missed appointment means the client has lost interest
in adoption. A phone call after a missed appointment is surely in order. Evening and weekend appointments are very helpful to those who have to lose
income when they take time off from work. An offer to meet the applicants
at their home, if that is preferred, is also very helpful. An appointment made
for the family's home is much less likely to be broken. In many ways a visit
to the family at their home is seen as a response honoring their desire to adopt
a waiting child.

> In one case, a Mr. and Mrs. A, calling in response to a TV presentation
> of a black fourteen-year-old, learning-disabled boy, began the adoption
> process with such a home visit. Later they said they would never have
> persisted had it not been for that initial home visit. (They adopted the
> boy they had called about, and he is doing well.)[24]

Anxiety about Adoption

It can be assumed that any person who applies to adopt feels extremely vulner-
able. Applicants know that in some way they are to be judged and fear they
may be found wanting.[25] One social worker has posed the problem of a judgmental approach this way:

> They come in and tell us that they have heard that we have been adver-
> tising for homes, that they want to have a child, and that the people in
> the neighborhood can attest to what good parents they would be. Then
> we given them the third degree.[26]

People react differently to anxiety. A middle-class person might react by
complaining to the agency head; a working-class person is more likely to just
give up and drop out. The problem is even greater when the client is black and
the worker is white. When black working-class applicants drop out because of
anxiety and lack of understanding about the adoption process, many good potential adoptive families are lost.[27] Social workers can help reduce the anxiety by
not using a judgmental approach, by letting clients know the different steps in

the adoption process, and by explaining the reasons for any delays.[28] Such careful explanations also help clear up any misconceptions the clients have about what will happen.

The Working Class and Official Documents

If they do not have them, working-class applicants may need help in getting birth, divorce, and death certificates or their legal substitutes. This is an area where workers particularly need to express a willingness to help, or else qualified applicants will disappear, assuming they cannot meet agency documentation requirements.

Black Client's Distrust

After having dealt with their own prejudices and lack of flexibility across racial and class lines, white social workers have to face the problem of building trust with the black clients and persuading them that they really are interested in serving blacks. The black applicant with a white worker often expects to be rejected. Black applicants have had other negative experiences with white professionals, and the black applicants wonder whether their chances are good enough to be worth the pain of subjecting themselves to judgment by a white in yet another area of their lives.[29]

The black applicants' suspicions affect the way a message is interpreted. For example, white applicants, told by a white social worker that there must be a four-month delay in the home study, may be very unhappy about the delay but accept it and wait out the four months. Black applicants, given the same message in the same tone of voice by the same white social worker, probably would react differently. To them it would probably carry the message that blacks are not welcome at this agency.

If they have a preference, black clients may feel reluctant to discuss their preference in skin color for their adopted child with a white worker. Black clients living in working-class black neighborhoods may be hesitant about agreeing to a home visit because they are apprehensive about the white social worker's reaction to their modest home or the neighborhood.[30]

And, in general, a number of black clients are anxious that white workers will have excessively high standards. One black client put it this way:

> We were apprehensive at the beginning that this person would come in
> and say "your apartment isn't big enough," or "you have too many bills,"
> or "you must stay home." Now I think it doesn't make much difference,
> but I think most black couples have the same apprehension.

Another said,

> We felt that black workers would be more sympathetic and wouldn't be
> looking for the same things that maybe a white worker would be look-
> ing for—such as a large income or an extra bedroom, which we didn't
> have. No, I just felt that we could express ourselves better, that she
> wouldn't, as I said before, be looking for the same things as a white
> worker would be looking for and she would understand that a black
> family maybe with three children would share and we wouldn't have a
> large house, which we didn't have at the time.

A social worker with a negative attitude can have quite an impact on black
applicants.

> The [first] interview was so horrendous, so frightening and intimidating
> that we changed our minds and it took a whole year before we tried
> again to adopt. I had wanted to adopt since I was fifteen years old. My
> mother had a lot of children, and I didn't want to have children of my
> own. The lady that we had the interview with questioned us in a very
> authoritative manner. We could accept the questions; it was the way
> she made us feel. After the discussion about fertility she said I was prob-
> ably having ideas that I would be doing some child a favor, and I should
> think about it.

> A year or two later, this couple approached another agency, prepared to
> suffer through the process. They adopted a little girl.[31]

In a study of almost 400 applicants to eight New York agencies, Bradley
found that the variables most highly associated with the case workers' perception
of couples as good prospects for adoption were variables which included the idea
of openness and communicativeness.[32] Yet precisely these characteristics are
the ones most likely to be missing in the interaction of white social workers and
black clients.

The black clients, abused in the past by discrimination, are likely to be more
cautious about what they say to white workers than black workers. White
workers may not understand this. As one observer has pointed out,

> I think that many times a faulty interpretation is made of the so-called
> inability of blacks to get on a "feeling level" as though this was a per-
> sonal defect rather than seeing it as the reluctance of blacks to express
> their feelings to a white person that they don't know.[33]

One black adoptive parent reported how difficult it was for him to have an
application interview with a white worker: ". . . and tell her all your business.
You feel as if she is prying. One just talks better to his own kind."[34] In the
black community a great deal of emphasis is placed on privacy and "staying out

of other people's business." This makes it even more difficult to disclose private matters to a stranger in an evaluative role.[35]

Many working-class and even middle-class black families are only a generation or less away from rock-bottom poverty. Clinical probing into this past by a middle-class white may be hurtful and unnecessary and may alienate people. Questions that deal with the here and now, examining the applicants in their current lives and giving full recognition to their current economic status, are more appropriate and more acceptable to clients.[36]

Whether because they feel a black social worker is less likely to be prejudiced, more likely to have reasonable standards, or more likely to understand them, some blacks in a variety of settings have expressed a preference for black social workers and black counselors. In a study using black interviewers, 500 ghetto residents were asked whether they preferred a black or white social worker. About 10 percent preferred a black worker. In a Chicago study, also using black interviewers, over half of the 291 respondents preferred a black caseworker. In a survey of New York City college students from poverty backgrounds, about one-fourth said they preferred a counselor of their racial background.[37] No comparable survey has been done in the area of adoptions, but studies such as reported in chapter 3 suggest that some black applicants do "vote with their feet" and drop out.

In the New York City Division of Adoption Services in 1972, at the time the cases reported in chapter 3 were processed, 89 percent of the adoption workers were white. In Washington, D.C., and Baltimore in 1970, when the data reported in chapter 2 were collected, 86 percent of the social workers were white. There is no evidence to suggest that the situation in other parts of the country has been much different in recent times. Indeed, a 1972 survey of a number of the agencies most interested in black adoptions in the United States showed that few of the workers, even in these agencies, were black. The vast majority of agencies, those without special emphasis on black adoptions, undoubtedly had even fewer black social workers or no black social workers at all.[38]

Guidelines for Improvement

The point is not that all black clients have to have black social workers. Rather, having black workers in an agency helps establish trust, persuading black applicants that the agency is sincere in wanting to provide adoptive service to blacks.[39] Black staff are especially important in promotional and educational campaigns. (Black foster parents can help in this area also.)

White workers need to begin to deal with their own prejudices and racial attitudes.[40] White workers need to learn:

To appreciate the pride black community members take in themselves as black people

To accept the legitimate claim of black Americans to different lifestyles

To recognize the strengths of black families

To appreciate the black community's drive to take responsibility for the things which affect their lives

To understand black attitudes toward "the establishment" and toward social agencies as part of the establishment, without becoming defensive

To observe all formalities that are overt indications of respect (rituals and forms are not empty gestures to people who have been insulted by their denial)[41]

To discuss race—to be "color blind" is to deny real differences

To become familiar with black culture and black history

To learn to understand the language of the ghetto[42]

Dealing with their own prejudices and racial attitudes is often very difficult and threatening for white workers because they have an emotional and professional stake in being able to establish rapport across racial lines. In fact, white workers can work well with black clients, but they do it so much more effectively after they have taken advantage of workshops and sensitivity training programs. Day-to-day discussions with black social workers who are coworkers also help.[43]

Notes

1. Crawford E. Burns, "White Staff, Black Children: Is There a Problem?" *Child Welfare* February 1971, pp. 90-96. Alfred Kadushin, "The Racial Factor in the Interview," *Social Work* May 1972, pp. 88-98. George P. Banks, "The Effects of Race on One-to-One Helping Interviews," *Social Science Review* June 1971, pp. 137-146. Dorcas Bowles, "Making Casework Relevant to Black People: Approaches, Techniques, Theoretical Implications," *Child Welfare* October 1969, pp. 468-475. Marylou Kincaid, "Identity and Therapy in the Black Community," *Personnel and Guidance Journal* May 1969, pp. 884-890. Jean Gochros, "Recognition and Use of Anger in Negro Clients," *Social Work* January 1966, pp. 28-38. Clemmont Vontross, "Counseling Blacks," *Personnel and Guidance Journal* May 1970, pp. 713-719; "Cultural Barriers in Counseling Relationships," *Personnel and Guidance Journal* September 1969, pp. 11-16; and "Racial Differences—Impediments to Rapport," *Journal of Counseling Psychology* January 1971, pp. 7-13.

2. For a discussion of black linquistic phenomena and black cultural norms associated with them, see William Labov, *Language in the Inner City: Studies in the Black English Vernacular* (Philadelphia: University of Pennsylvania Press, 1972); J.L. Dillard, *Black English* (New York: Random House, 1972); Jim Haskins and Hugh F. Butts, *The Psychology of Black Language* (New York: Harper & Row, 1973); John Horton, "Time and Cool People," *Trans-Action Magazine* April 1967; Thomas Kochman, ed., *Rappin' and Stylin' Out* (Urbana: University of Illinois Press, 1972); Thomas Kochman, "Toward an Ethnography of Black American Speech Behavior," *Afro-American Anthropology,* eds. Whitten and Szwed (New York: Macmillan, 1970); and Dorothy Z. Seymour, "Black Children, Black Language," *Washington Post* June 25, 1972.

3. Elizabeth Herzog, Cecelia Sudia, Jane Harwood, and Carol Newcomb, *Families for Black Children* (Washington: Government Printing Office, 1971), p. 32; and Emelicia Mizio, "White Worker–Minority Client," *Social Work* May 1972, pp. 82-86. In the course of preparing this study, two fine illustrations of cultural misunderstandings came to my attention. One—Burns, "White Staff, Black Children," pp. 90-96—dealt with black-white misunderstandings in an area other than adoptions.

Some black children at Children's Village, an institutional home for children, had Vaseline in their lockers. It was discovered and taken away by white staff, who were concerned about possible homosexual activities. The psychiatrist learned that the boys were worried about ashy skin, a blemish experienced by some blacks during the winter. The Vaseline was being used to grease their skin, but the boys had not wanted to tell this to white staff.

The other illustration deals with cross-cultural misunderstandings between white adoption workers and Spanish-speaking clients (see Phyllis Dunne, "Placing Children of Minority Groups for Adoption," *Children* March-April 1958, p. 47):

We have had to remain aware of the differences in family relationships in various cultures. The Caucasian couple who brings the husband's mother to the intake interview may raise some questions in the worker's mind: Is this man so dependent upon his mother? What is the marital relationship here? However, some cultures still fully accept the matriarch, who is loved and respected. If such an important figure exists in a family being considered as a permanent one for a child, it is important that she, as the grandmother-to-be, understands what is going on and is included in this study.

4. New York State Adoption Service, *Manual on Adoption Services: Recruitment and Adoption Study Process,* 1978, p. 19, and personal communication from Leora Neal, head of the National Association of Black Social Workers Child Adoption and Referral Service of New York.

5. Black Child Development Institute, "That They May Have Homes: A Report of the Black Child Advocacy Adoption Project" (Washington, 1974), p. 9.

6. New York State Adoption Service, *Manual on Adoption Services*, p. 18.

7. "Adoption," *The Black Child Advocate* 5, no. 5 (1977): 4, special issue.

8. Ibid.

9. Ibid. Reprinted with permission.

10. Stephen Baratz and Joan Baratz, "The Social Pathology Model: Historical Bases for Psychology's Denial of the Existence of Negro Culture" (Paper presented at the meetings of the American Psychological Association in 1969). Robert Staples, "Toward a Sociology of the Black Family: A Theoretical and Methodological Assessment," *A Decade of Family Research and Action*, ed. C.B. Broderick (Minneapolis: National Council on Family Relations, 1971), pp. 141-160. Albert Murray, "White Norms, Black Deviation," *The Death of White Sociology*, ed. Joyce A. Ladner (New York: Random House, 1973).

11. Julia B. Bloch, "The White Worker and the Negro Client in Psychotherapy," *Social Work* April 1968, p. 38; Burns, "White Staff, Black Children," p. 93.

12. Inez L. Gibbs, "Institutional Racism in Social Welfare," *Child Welfare* 10, no. 10 (1971): 585; and Bloch, "The White Worker and the Negro Client in Psychotherapy," p. 40.

13. A 1971 conference on adoption attended by social workers from the District of Columbia and attended by the author.

14. My thanks to Carol Williams of the University of Southern California for suggesting this point.

15. Mizio, "White Worker–Minority Client," p. 84f.

16. Ibid.

17. Herzog et al., *Families for Black Children* p. 20; and Annie Lee Sandusky, Jane Harwood Rea, Ursula Gallagher, and Elizabeth Herzog, *Families for Black Children* (Washington: Government Printing Office, 1972), p. 6.

18. Christopher Unger, Gladys Dwarshuis, and Elizabeth Johnson, *Chaos, Madness, and Unpredictability . . . Placing the Child with Ears Like Uncle Harry's* (Chelsea, Mich.: Spaulding for Children, 1977), p. 187. Reprinted with permission.

19. Ibid., pp. 187-194.

20. Herzog et al., *Families for Black Children*, p. 19.

21. Ibid., p. 25.

22. Unger, Dwarshuis, and Johnson, *Chaos, Madness, and Unpredictability*, pp. 188-190. Reprinted with permission.

23. New York State Adoption Service, *Manual on Adoption Services*, p. 19; and Dunne, "Placing Children of Minority Groups for Adoption," p. 47f.

24. Ibid., p. 12. Reprinted with permission.

25. Herzog et al., *Families for Black Children,* p. 16.

26. Ibid., p. 29.

27. Clarence D. Fischer, "Homes for Black Children," *Child Welfare* February 1971, p. 111; and D. Middelstadt, E. Kenyon, R.D. Stahlke, and F.A. Matzke, "Adoption Counseling—New Opportunity for Growth," *Child Welfare* 46, no. 7 (1967): 365-370, 385.

28. New York State Adoption Service, *Manual on Adoption Services,* p. 24.

29. Mizio, "White Worker—Minority Client," p. 83; Mildred Hawkins, "Negro Adoptions—Challenge Accepted," *Child Welfare* December 1960, p. 23; and New York State Adoption Service, *Manual on Adoption Services,* p. 18.

30. Dunne, "Placing Children of Minority Groups for Adoption," p. 47f.

31. New York State Adoption Service, *Manual on Adoption Services,* pp. 5, 11, 22. Reprinted with permission.

32. Trudy Bradley, *An Exploration of Caseworkers' Perceptions of Adoptive Applicants* (New York: Child Welfare League of America, 1967), p. 191; and Lela B. Costin, *Child Welfare: Policies and Practices,* ed. David Edwards (New York: McGraw-Hill, 1972).

33. Herzog et al., *Families for Black Children,* p. 32.

34. Kadushin, "The Racial Factor in the Interview," p. 88; and Martha Perry, "An Experiment in Recruitment of Negro Adoptive Parents," *Social Casework* May 1958, p. 294f.

35. My thanks to Carol Williams of the University of Southern California for suggesting this point.

36. New York State Adoption Service, *Manual on Adoption Services,* p. 18.

37. Sumati Dubey, "Blacks' Preference for Black Professionals, Businessmen and Religious Leaders," *Public Opinion Quarterly* Spring 1970, pp. 113-116. Donald Brieland, "Black Identity and the Helping Person," *Children* September-October 1969, pp. 172-174. Burton L. Backner, "Counseling Black Students: Any Place for Whitey?" *Journal of Higher Education* November 1970, pp. 630-637. Harvey R. St. Clare, "Psychiatric Interview Experiences with Negroes," *American Journal of Psychiatry* November 1951, pp. 113-119. Franklin T. Barrett and Felice Perlmutter, "Black Clients and White Workers: A Report from the Field," *Child Welfare* January 1972, pp. 19-24.

38. Annie Lee Sandusky, Jane Harwood Rea, Ursula Gallagher, and Elizabeth Herzog. *Families for Black Children: The Search for Adoptive Parents,* part II, "Programs and Projects" (Washington: Government Printing Office, 1972).

39. Esther Fibush, "The White Worker and the Negro Client," *Social Casework* May 1965, p. 273; and Sandusky et al., *Families for Black Children,* pp. 7, 30.

40. Mizio, "White Worker—Minority Client," p. 83. Bloch, "The White Worker and the Negro Client in Psychotherapy," p. 39, provides an interesting example of what happened following the admission of black children to a

residential treatment center under Jewish auspices:

> A sudden "color blindness" seemed to have beset the total staff. Only
> upon specific inquiry did they report that some white children had
> reacted angrily to the acceptance of the Negro child. Their reports lacked
> the usual astute observation in this area. Nor did they report anything
> about their own feelings and reactions. There was a period of denial of
> difference.

Copyright 1968, National Association of Social Workers, Inc. Reprinted with
permission from *Social Work* April 1968, pp. 36–42. See also Joe Yamamoto,
"Factors in Patient Selection," *American Journal of Psychiatry* November 1967,
pp. 630–636.

   41. Bloch, "The White Worker and the Negro Client in Psychotherapy,"
p. 37, provides an instructive example:

> Mr. F, a black college graduate and teacher, objected to his worker's
> addressing him by his first name; he saw in this a reflection of white
> condescension toward him as a black person. The therapist, a psycho-
> analyst, assured him that he did not share such attitudes and used the
> first name with all his patients. As a result of the therapist's continued
> use of his first name, the patient withdrew from treatment, although
> he was later able to establish a positive relationship with another white
> mental health worker.

Copyright 1968, National Association of Social Workers, Inc. Reprinted with
permission from *Social Work* April 1968, pp. 36–42.

   42. Kadushin, 1972, "The Racial Factor in the Interview," p. 91.
   43. Burns, "White Staff, Black Children," p. 94; and Esther Fibush and
BeAlva Turnquest, "A Black and White Approach to the Problem of Racism,"
Social Casework October 1970, p. 466; Sandusky et al., *Families for Black
Children*, p. 7; and Child Welfare League of America, *Standards for Adoption
Service* (New York, 1973), p. 92.

5

Unavoidable Mistakes and Self-Interest

Our two adopted children arrived with a multitude of emotional scars, open wounds, and learning problems. My background in professional social work was invaluable in helping us recognize problem areas and get appropriate help. After three years filled with therapy and training, I now sometimes dare to believe that we all might survive as one family. I still believe in adoption, but the concept has lost its sparkle—and has caused much pain and much guilt, although the odds seem at last to be evening out—and for that I'm grateful.[1]

* * *

When our oldest daughter (now 13) was placed in our home at age 9, she was quite withdrawn—a "good" girl who did not know how to express her feelings, especially negative feelings of anger, fear, frustration, and disappointment. She had not cried in three years, and her only emotional reaction to stress was to vomit nightly at the dinner table.

At the time we adopted Julie, our youngest and only child was Chelle who was two years old. Julie saw that Chelle threw tantrums and was often less than loveable and that we did not get rid of her.

The first six months were rough. Once Julie began to cry, she cried over everything. She also threw temper tantrums, stamped her feet, slammed doors, and was sure that we loved Chelle more than we loved her. Paul and I began to question whether we were the right family for Julie. She seemed so unhappy, and nothing we did seemed to satisfy her.

We sought help from the Older Child Group of COAC, our adoptive parents group, and from a clinic recommended by our social worker. The head of the Older Child Group calmed us; just knowing that our doubts and fears were not strange or unique helped us feel less anxious. The clinic's evaluation showed no major problems other than a basic insecurity and poor self-image, problems to be expected in a child when her original family had been scattered and she had been moved from place to place.

After five months of therapy, Julie and her counselor decided that she didn't need it any more. Once we began adoption proceedings, Julie was fine. She knew that she was going to stay with us and that we would accept her even when she wasn't "good."

The second older child that came to live with us was an eight-year-old boy who had been living in a residential treatment center since age five. Our social worker helped us with the placement (we had found the child ourselves) but cautioned us that he was different than Julie, that this child was quite disturbed. We said, "Sure, sure—all any child needs is love and attention to straighten him out."

This time we did not wait six months to get help but immediately looked into special schools, therapy programs, and parent groups. We did make progress and there were some good times, but finally, after two years of intense physical and emotional energy, the people at the mental health clinic forced us to sit down and evaluate the situation. Yes, there had been improvement, but was it enough? Did we think things were going to change for the better? If not, could we live with the situation as it was? Were we asking an emotional commitment from this child that he simply could not give? Would he, really, be happier in a residential treatment center, in a setting that gave him limits but did not demand that he form close personal relationships with people? Was it fair to us or to our other children to spend almost all our time and energy on one member of the family?

I am extremely grateful to the mental health people and to our social worker (who did not say, "I told you so") for the support and understanding they gave us as we made the decision to give up this child. His disturbance could not be "fixed"—at least not by us.

I am more realistic now. My husband and I have learned our strengths and weaknesses. We are still optimistic about disturbed children and feel that every child deserves a chance with a loving, committed family, a flexible school system, and supportive community services.[2]

Adoptions which fail are very difficult for the family, the child, and the social worker who made the placement. Fortunately, adoption failure—the return of the child to the agency—happens very seldom. Eight studies involving the placement of almost 35,000 children showed an average failure rate of less than 2 percent.

In a study of close to 3000 placements made by a Wisconsin agency between 1960 and 1967, Kadushin and Seidl found an overall failure rate of slightly less than 3 percent. The failure rate for children under age 2 was 1 percent; for children aged 2 to 6, 7 percent; and for children aged 6 and over, 9 percent. Half the returned children were successfully replaced in other adoptive homes.[3]

Spaulding for Children, a Michigan agency specializing in the adoption of physically handicapped, retarded, and emotionally disturbed children, had a disruption (failure) rate of about 11 percent for the years between 1968 and 1976. Of 21 children involved in the disruptions, 19 were placed with other adoptive families. Of the 2 who were not replaced, 1 (a teenager) chose to live semi-independently with his grandmother. The other, an 11-year-old boy who had had a total of four disrupted adoptions, was placed in a group home, since he apparently could not manage close family relationships.[4]

An Ohio adoption project, trained in the Spaulding techniques and also specializing in the very hard-to-place child, had a disruption rate of 14 percent during its period of operation between 1975 and 1977.[5]

No statistics exist on the failure rate of black adoptions. However, it seems reasonable that the failure rate parallels that for adopted children of all races and that the placement of black infants is a much less risky affair than the placement of black children who are older or who have physical or emotional handicaps.

The failure rate for older children is understandable. The parents have to adjust to an already-existing personality: the child has previous attachments and certain expectations about what his or her parents will be like. Clashes can be expected, and sometimes the individuals involved may feel the differences are insurmountable.

The physically handicapped child brings all the problems of adjusting to that handicap. The child who is retarded or emotionally disturbed places other burdens on the adopting parents. Here, again, it is easy to see why some people will try their best and then decide they simply cannot manage.

What is remarkable with these complex adoptions is that the success rate is so high. A failure rate of 10 to 15 percent means that 85 to 90 percent of the adoptions are succeeding!

Adoption Failure Is Unavoidable

Is there a way to eliminate the failures? The staff at Spaulding for Children, experts on placement of the hard-to-place, think not. It is inevitable that some children will be returned, they feel, because social workers can never learn enough about a child and a family to be able to defuse or eliminate all potentially disruptive problems. Careful preparation of both the child and adoptive parents is necessary and appropriate. But after a certain point, the risk must be taken. According to Spaulding staff,

> If a worker is convinced all disruptions are avoidable, that worker may spend an inordinate amount of time attempting to identify and eliminate possible causes for disruption. Applicants may be intensely scrutinized and, in some cases, may even be rejected simply because they have a single characteristic in common with a family whose adoption disrupted. However, such devoted scrutiny will only increase worker anxiety, for despite the most profound effort, disruptions will continue to occur.[6]

The Spaulding staff shares placement decisions and disruption decisions, thus providing strong support to the individual worker involved directly with the child and family.[7]

As their replacement figures indicate, Spaulding sees the disrupted adoption as the product of a unique set of circumstances and not a statement that either the child or the family are incapable of adoption. In their study of a Wisconsin agency Kadushin and Seidl take the same position.[8]

As Spaulding staff see the situation,

Workers must take risks, live with difficulties, and look for parents who can do the same. They must realize that unless they run the risks of an adoptive placement, the child's chances for permanence are zero.[9]

The Spaulding for Children staff have learned that many working-class people are better able to accept the disabilities of the hard-to-place child than many middle-class people are. Thus Spaulding training for new staff includes material sensitizing the adoption workers to effective ways of establishing rapport with working-class clients.[10]

Professional Leadership and Black Adoptions

Spaulding leadership has not been as sensitive to the problems of working across racial lines as they have to the problems of working across class lines. This is partly the outgrowth of the particular situation in Michigan. A very fine black adoption agency, Homes for Black Children of Detroit, was located near the original Spaulding agency. (There are now several Spaulding agencies.) And thus Spaulding referred many black children and clients to Homes for Black Children instead of providing service themselves. This may have been appropriate in the Michigan context, but the result was the Spaulding staff never developed an understanding of the problems which can arise between white staff and black clients.[11] Now Spaulding staff, through the financial support of the Edna McConnell Clark Foundation, are moving into training social workers at a number of different agencies across the United States.[12]

There is evidence that at least some white Spaulding staff work well across racial lines. But until there is a willingness to acknowledge explicitly that white workers can have problems establishing a trusting relationship with black clients, the Spaulding training will be missing an important component.

In the course of preparing this book, I spoke with a number of white professionals who had not thought about the problems black clients have with white social workers. A classic exchange occurred when I asked a woman in charge of a training program for adoption workers whether she planned to include material on this issue. Her response was, "Well, there *shouldn't* be any problem" (italics added).

The Impact of the Profession on Black Adoptions in Washington, D.C., and Baltimore

The problem of the leadership in the social work profession ignoring or denying problems with respect to black adoptions is not new. At the time data were collected for the study reported in chapter 2, the influence of the social work

profession on black adoptions was also explored. It had been expected that contact with the social work profession would have a positive influence—that white
social workers in contact with the profession would be more knowledgeable
about ways of attracting black applicants and working with black clients, and
consequently that the agencies of professionally oriented social workers would
be more involved with black placements. The exact opposite turned out to be
the case. The more professionally oriented an agency's white social workers
were, the less likely the agency was to be making a large percentage of its placements with black adopters (table 5-1).

Contact with the social work profession was measured in terms of

1. Membership in professional organizations (the percentage of white workers
    who reported belonging to any professional organization);
2. Attendance at professional meetings (the percentage of white workers who
    had attended two or more professional meetings in the past);
3. Whether the worker's most important source of information on new things
    in adoptions was outside the agency (the percentage of white workers who
    reported that their most important source of information on new things in
    the field of adoption was outside the agency).

Those who looked outside their own agency for new ideas in adoptions presumably had more professional contact than those who just talked to people inside
their own agency.

No matter how professional contact was measured, the outcome was the
same: greater professional contact by white workers meant proportionately
fewer agency placements with black adopters. Could this relationship, as it
appeared, be misleading, explainable by other variables? Several other variables
were tried as controls:

1. The percentage of the agency's social workers who had a master's degree in
    social work
2. Agency size measured in terms of the number of professionals employed
3. The percentage of the people in the agency's constituency who were black
4. The source of operating funds for the agency (whether the funds came
    from a United Fund, other private sources, or tax monies)

As each of these variables was added as a control, the initial correlation did fall
somewhat. But on the whole, the strong negative relationship between professional contact by white social workers and placements with black adopters
remained.

For most of the relationships examined, the correlation coefficients
declined somewhat when we shifted from placements in 1970 to placements

Table 5-1

Zero- and First-Order Partial Correlations between Indicators of Professional
Contact and Percentage of Agency Placements Made with Black Adopters,
Washington, D.C., and Baltimore, 1970 and 1971

Indicators of Professional Contact by White Workers[a]	Adoptions by Blacks	
	1970	1971
Look outside organization for news[b]	−.74	−.75
Controlling for[c]		
Workers with master's degrees[d]	−.77	−.75
Number of professionals	−.63	−.62
Percentage of territory black	−.68	−.62
Community funding	−.75	−.74
Attended two or more professional meetings[b]	−.63	−.50
Controlling for[c]		
Workers with master's degrees[d]	−.63	−.50
Number of professionals	−.53	−.34
Percentage of territory black	−.57	−.40
Community funding	−.65	−.49
Member professional organization[b]	−.63	−.44
Controlling for[c]		
Workers with master's degrees[d]	−.73	−.59
Number of professionals	−.49	−.19
Percentage of territory black	−.64	−.49
Community funding	−.54	−.42

Source: District of Columbia and Baltimore Adoption Agency Survey.

[a]The percentage base for these variables is the total number of agency social workers, both
black and white. The numerator is the number of white workers who reported the particular
kind of professional contact.

[b]Zero-order correlations.

[c]First-order partial correlations. See chapter 2 for details on the construction of the variables labeled: number of professionals, percentage of territory black, and community
funding.

[d]Coefficients in these rows are based on data from 16 agencies. In the other rows, coefficients are based on data from 17 agencies. This is a study of a population, not a sample.
However, for those accustomed to evaluating coefficients in terms of statistical significance,
it may be useful to know that, if this had been a sample, all the coefficients with an absolute
value higher than .41 had a probability of less than 1 in 20 of occurring by chance.

in 1971. However, even after the decline, the negative relationship between professional contacts and black placements remained.

When the correlations were run using the professional contact scores of
black workers and white workers combined, the negative correlation fell, indicating that for black workers contact with the profession was not associated with
less involvement in black adoptions.[13]

How could contact with the social work profession have had such a negative impact on white social workers? To answer that question, let us consider the content of the adoption literature during the 1960s, the period just preceding the time when the Washington, D.C., and Baltimore data were collected.[14]

The Adoption Literature and Blacks

Most of the adoption literature in the 1960s did not deal with the adoption of black children at all. It dealt with other issues—the problem of the mentally retarded, independent adoptions, the unmarried father, and so on. Many of these topics could apply to black children and black adopters as well as white; but as the topics were treated in the literature, they did not.[15]

Of the literature which did deal explicitly with black adoptions, one can identify two distinct streams. One was the how-to literature. This literature was written almost entirely by social work practitioners actively involved in black adoptions. Within their writings (which go back at least as far as the early 1950s), one finds a remarkable convergence in practice. The social workers were agreed on the extreme importance of both agency outreach and sympathetic processing in recruiting black adopters.

The other distinct stream of thought is less closely tied to practice. Beginning with the observation that very few black people were adopting children through agencies, the writers in this stream tried to explain why this was so. Using studies done by Deasy and Quinn and Fowler, the writers argued that middle-class blacks were not interested in adopting.[16] Statistics published by Herzog and Bernstein suggested that if one looked only at adoptions among the middle class, blacks appeared to be adopting in greater numbers than whites.[17] The conclusion drawn was that the agencies were not responsible for the fact that there were so few black adopters. The fault lay within the black community itself—the low incomes and the lack of motivation to adopt.

Subsequent research has challenged the accuracy of the methodology and conclusions of the Deasy and Quinn and Fowler research, and a reexamination of the statistics utilized in the Herzog and Bernstein research leads one to question the conclusions of that article as well.[18] But for our present purposes, the important point is that during the late 1960s there existed a fairly sophisticated rationale for explaining the small numbers of black adopters in terms of a lack of interest and inability within the black community. The agencies themselves did not need to change.[19]

Thus the workers looking for a justification for inactivity in black adoptions could easily have found it in the literature of the 1960s.[20] Those who were neutral also probably would have concluded that substantial numbers of black adoptions were not possible. It is likely that only those with a special interest in black adoptions sought out the encouraging how-to literature.

Communication and Risk

By the mid-1970s the content of the adoption literature had changed. Proportionately more black children were being placed, so more and more social
workers were realizing that black adopters could be found. But still one finds
a reluctance on the part of some white social workers to become involved in
black adoptions. The reasons are related to communication problems and the
fears adoption workers have of being involved in an adoption which fails.

Many social workers are not aware of the insight of the Spaulding agencies
that some adoption failures are unavoidable. As a result, the adoption workers
focus too much on the specter of the disrupted adoption. Since all adoption
workers share this problem, the anxieties of the workers reenforce one another.
The criteria for adoptive parenthood get narrower and narrower as the workers
strive to avoid the unavoidable. Clients from another cultural group who are
difficult to understand, clients who are not able to express their feelings easily,
and clients who do not quickly develop a trust of the worker are all encouraged
to drop out. With the best of intentions, that of avoiding a placement which
fails, the workers make another mistake—that of rejecting good applicants.

When the social worker is white and the applicants are black, the communication problems can be quite serious. When the social worker is white and
middle-class and the client is black and working-class, the communication problems can be even more serious. The response of the social workers is key. If
workers accept that establishing good rapport is their responsibility, the problem may be overcome. If workers take a cautious, risk-avoiding course and
assume that noncommunicative (to them) black applicants are not ready to
adopt, good applicants will be encouraged to drop out. (For a discussion of
how applicants are encouraged to drop out, see chapter 3.)

Difficulties in communication cause workers to raise their standards for
adoptive parenthood. It works this way. When workers feel comfortable with
their clients, a working mother may seem quite acceptable. When workers feel
uncomfortable, a mother who plans to work may seem too risky. When workers
feel comfortable with their clients, a relatively low income may not seem to be
a serious obstacle to adoption. When workers feel uncomfortable, a low income
may make adoption seem questionable. As was shown in chapter 3, communication problems with these unfortunate outcomes occur more frequently with
white workers and black clients than with black workers and black clients (see
table 3-6).

Difficulties in communication can cause a worker to delay, simply to have
more time to make a decision. As was pointed out in chapter 4, black clients of
white workers tend to interpret delays negatively, even when the delays are not
so intended.

Some social workers judge parenting capacity by the applicants' ability to
stick it out through a difficult adoption process. This approach may be followed

with the best of intentions, but the good intentions do not mitigate its ill effects on black applicants. (Social workers who try to substitute tenacity in the application process for evaluating adoptive parenthood are not alone. Other professionals in uncertain situations have also tried this approach, ineffective though it is.[21])

Altogether, communication problems and the fear of adoption failure come together to make black adoptions a high-risk activity for white workers. Using mass-media publicity to attract black applicants, if it is new to the adoption worker, adds yet another risk.

Self-Interest

Quite apart from risks and communication problems (as discussed in this chapter) and prejudice (as discussed in the previous chapter), certain other factors make having black clients seem disadvantageous.

1. A black home study may require more time if needed marriage, divorce, or birth certificates must be secured from some Southern states. This can be a problem for adoption workers whose productivity is measured by the number of applicant studies completed within a specified period.[22]

2. Having a number of black clients can lower agency income. Agencies with fees almost always have a sliding scale whereby those with lower incomes pay a reduced fee or no fee at all. This means that black clients, with their lower incomes, will be paying lower fees.[23]

3. When mass-media publicity is used to attract black applicants, the agency, right after the publicity, is flooded with applicants. Processing all the applicants within a reasonable time means more work for the social workers.[24]

4. To accommodate working-class clients, agencies need to institute evening and Saturday hours. This may not be convenient for the workers.

5. To work effectively with black clients, white workers have to learn more about black culture and to deal with their own prejudices. This is again more work. Having to deal with one's prejudices is also anxiety-provoking.

6. Working with black clients, particularly black working-class clients, can be seen as a lower-status activity. As a society, we have put legal segregation behind us, but vestiges of the frame of mind that created it continue. As a society, we also put a lesser value on people who work with their hands for wages. Together, this means that working with black working-class clients can be seen as a low-status activity. One wishes it were otherwise, but these status differences exist in the wider society and they affect social workers also.

For white social workers, then, greater involvement with black adopters means more risk, harder work, and lower status. As white workers deal with their own prejudices, hopefully the status loss through changing clientele becomes less important. As white workers become more familiar with black culture, the strain of working with clients of a different culture presumably decreases also. And with increased communication and rapport, making accurate judgments about a black couple's potential as adoptive parents is made easier and less risky. White social workers can work effectively with black clients, but doing so takes recognition of the potential problems and training and self-examination.

Notes

1. Nancy Tompkins and Mary Bailey, "A Dialogue about Adoption," *Friends Journal* 22 no. 13 ©1976. Reprinted with permission.

2. Janice Watkins, "The Emotionally Disturbed Older Child," D.C. COAC, Washington, D.C., December 1977, p. 9f. Reprinted with permission.

3. Alfred Kadushin and Frederick W. Seidl, "Adoption Failure: A Social Work Postmortem," *Social Work* July 1971, pp. 33-35, 38.

4. Christopher Unger, Gladys Dwarshuis, and Elizabeth Johnson, *Chaos, Madness, and Unpredictability . . . Placing the Child with Ears Like Uncle Harry's* (Chelsea, Mich.: Spaulding for Children, 1977), p. 218.

5. Barbara Roberts, "Ohio District 11 Adoption Project Final Report" (Report submitted to U.S. Department of Health, Education, and Welfare, Office of Child Development, February 1978), p. 25.

6. Unger, Dwarshuis, and Johnson, *Chaos, Madness, and Unpredictability*, p. 201. Reprinted with permission.

7. Ibid., p. 212.

8. Ibid., pp. 218-224. Kadushin and Seidl, "Adoption Failure," p. 38.

9. Unger, Dwarshuis, and Johnson, *Chaos, Madness, and Unpredictability*, p. 203. Reprinted with permission.

10. Ibid., chap. 13.

11. Unger, Dwarshuis, and Johnson's book, *Chaos, Madness and Unpredictability*, is an excellent, detailed how-to book on adoptions from the Spaulding point of view. Nowhere in it is there an acknowledgment of the difficulties that black clients can have with white social workers.

12. Ibid., pp. 299-310.

13. The work of Piven and Cloward in welfare and Stephenson in elementary education suggest that professionals are reluctant to take risks for black clients. Becker's work with health professions indicates that health administrators oriented toward their profession are unlikely to utilize high-risk innovations. Francis Fox Piven and Richard A. Cloward, *Regulating the Poor* (New York: Vintage Books, 1971). John S. Stephenson, "Professionalism and Innovation Acceptance among Teachers" (Ph.D. dissertation, Ohio State University, 1972). Marshall H. Becker, "Sociometric Location and Innovativeness: Reformulation and Extension of the Diffusion Model," *American Sociological Review* April 1970, pp. 267-282.

14. The published literature is taken as an indicator of the content of all professional discussions relating to adoptions.

15. Howard G. Aronson, "The Problem of Rejection of Adoptive Applicants," *Child Welfare,* October 1960, pp. 21-26. M.J. Began, "Mental Retardation: The Role of the Voluntary Social Agency," *Social Casework* 1964, pp. 457-464. Howard Bluth, "Factors in the Decision to Adopt Independently," *Child Welfare* November 1967, pp. 504-513. L.C. Burgess, "The Unmarried Father in Adoption Planning," *Children* 1968, pp. 71-74.

16. L.C. Deasy and Olive W. Quinn, "The Urban Negro and Adoption of Children," *Child Welfare* November 1962, pp. 400-407. Irving A. Fowler, "The Urban Middle-Class Negro and Adoption: Two Series of Studies and Their Implications for Action," *Child Welfare* November 1966, pp. 522-525. Robert G. Andrews, "Permanent Placement of Negro Children through Quasi-Adoption," *Child Welfare* December 1968, p. 583. Alfred Kadushin and Frederick W. Seidl, "Adoption Failures: A Social Work Postmortem," *Social Work* July 1971, p. 30.

17. Elizabeth Herzog and Rose Bernstein, "Why So Few Negro Adoptions?" *Children* January-February 1965, pp. 14-18. Andrews, "Permanent Placement of Negro Children through Quasi-Adoption," p. 583.

18. L.C. Deasy and J.W. Mullaney, "The Suburban White and the Adoption of Children," *Social Science Review* September 1970, pp. 275-284.

19. Andrews, "Permanent Placement of Negro Children through Quasi-Adoption," p. 583.

20. In his study of professionalism and social worker activism, Epstein found that a professional orientation intensified the basic commitments the social workers already had; in other words, those who were conservative and had a professional orientation were more likely to behave in a conservative way than those who were conservative but did not have the professional orientation. Similarly, those who were more radical and had a professional commitment were more likely to behave in a radical way than those who were radical but did not have a professional orientation. Our speculation is that professional orientation could act on racial biases in exactly this same way. See Irwin Epstein, "Professional Role Orientations and Conflict Strategies," *Social Work* October 1970, pp. 87-92.

21. Alvin W. Gouldner, "The Secrets of Organization," in *The Social Welfare Forum: 1963,* National Conference on Social Welfare Official Proceedings, 1963 (New York: Columbia University Press, 1963), p. 172. James D. Thompson, *Organizations in Action* (New York: McGraw-Hill, 1967), p. 87. Peter M. Blau and Richard Scott, *Formal Organizations: A Comparative Approach* (San Francisco: Chandler, 1962), p. 247. Don H. Zimmerman, "Record-Keeping and the Intake Process in a Public Welfare Agency," *On Record: Files and Dossiers in American Life,* ed. Stanton Wheeler (New York: Russell Sage Foundation, 1969), pp. 319-354.

22. Annie Lee Sandusky, Jane Harwood Rea, Ursula Gallagher, and

Elizabeth Herzog, *Families for Black Children,* Part II, "Programs and Projects" (Washington: Government Printing Office, 1972), p. 13.

23. Black Child Development Institute, *Black Child Advocate: Adoption,* 5, no. 5 (1977): 5, special issue.

24. Elizabeth Herzog, Cecelia Sudia, Jane Harwood, and Carol Newcomb, *Families for Black Children: An Experience Survey* (Washington: Government Printing Office, 1971), p. 51.

6 Whites Adopting Black Children

By the end of 1977 about 15,000 black children had been adopted by whites.[1] Instances of whites adopting black children have been reported as early as 1948 in Minnesota, 1952 in New York, 1954 in Georgia, and 1955 in California. Since interracial adoption was illegal in Georgia until the late 1960s and obstructed even after that, the 1954 adoption was informal and did not go through the courts.[2]

Why did these interracial adoptions occur? Until the 1960s segregation was common in hotels, restaurants, and bus station waiting rooms. In the early 1960s blacks and whites were killed when they tried to help Southern blacks register to vote. Even in the 1970s segregated schools, neighborhoods, and hospitals continue to exist.

The story of the continuing discrimination is so well known that one almost forgets that there is another tradition as well—that some whites have always fought against racial oppression and that other whites have let their lives become entwined with those of black people and shared some of their burdens.

Interracial Marriage

The antimiscegenation laws—laws prohibiting marriage between whites and blacks—were not passed to protect black slave women from sexual exploitation by their white owners. The laws were "necessary" only because some whites and blacks loved one another as equals and wanted to marry.

The antimiscegenation laws of colonial times were enacted in Northern states such as Massachusetts and Pennsylvania as well as in the South. There were penalties. In Virginia, for example, for blacks held in slavery, the prohibition against marrying a white person was part of the general prohibition against marrying at all. Free black women and white men suffered the same limitation—not being permitted to marry if the person they wished to marry was of another race. But they could have children together. The "crime" of the white women was more conspicuous and was not ignored. The white woman who had a brown-skinned child immediately lost her child. The child was indentured until age 25 or 31. The white mother herself was indentured for a term of five or six years. All this was recorded in the court records of Virginia as indentured mulatto children, fully grown, petitioned for their freedom.[3]

Over the years, the antimiscegenation laws and their penalties varied. Just before World War II, 31 states still had antimiscegenation laws. These slowly were repealed by the state legislatures. For some states the changes occurred quite late—Nevada, Idaho, and California in 1958 and Arizona in 1959. By 1967, 17 states still had antimiscegenation laws. In Delaware the crime invited a fine of $100 or imprisonment for thirty days. In Georgia there was no fine, but the offending couple could be imprisoned, separately of course, for one to two years. In Mississippi the penalty was most severe, with the possibility of imprisonment for up to ten years.

Under the United States Constitution, marriage is a matter for state law. And the states have generally respected one another's laws so that, for example, a couple legally married in one state was legally married in all the other states also. Not so with interracial marriages. A black person and a white person legally married in one state could move to another state and suddenly find themselves subject to criminal penalties. This anomolous situation finally ended in 1967 when the U.S. Supreme Court, in an unambiguous decision, declared that the antimiscegenation laws were unconstitutional. The case precipitating the judgment had involved an interracial couple appropriately surnamed Loving.[4]

Legal Status of Interracial Adoption

Following the Supreme Court decision on interracial marriage, states with anti-miscegenation laws still on the books began removing them. Adoption laws were also revised in this period, so that by mid-1978 only eight states had laws relating to adoption which mentioned race.[5] And of those eight, only three— Georgia, Michigan, and South Carolina—mentioned race as a criterion for determining the suitability of particular parents as adopters of a particular child. The Georgia and Michigan statutes do not refer to particular racial groups.[6] The South Carolina statute does; it permits whites to adopt black children and explicitly prevents blacks from adopting white children:

> It shall be unlawful for any parent, relative or other white person in this State, having the control or custody of any white child by right of guardianship, natural or acquired or otherwise, to dispose of, give or surrender such white child permanently into the custody, control, maintenance or support of a Negro. Any person violating the provisions of this section shall be guilty of a misdemeanor and on conviction, shall be fined or imprisoned, in the discretion of the presiding judge.[7]

Three states—Indiana, Oklahoma, and Pennsylvania—direct the courts to keep a record of the race of the child only.[8] South Dakota directs the courts to keep a record of the race of both the child and the adoption petitioners.[9] Only one state—Kentucky—actually forbids adoption agencies from denying an adoption on the basis of race.[10]

Although most state adoption statutes do not focus on race, many adoption agencies and judges still do. Up to a point, such a focus is sensible. White children are almost always placed with white families. If black adoptive homes are available, black children should be placed with them.

But what seems sensible as a general rule can become quite absurd when applied to particular circumstances. Consider these examples:[a]

> Mr. and Mrs. John Jones, a Georgia couple, took adoptive custody of a little girl when she was three days old, told that her father was Italian. Nine months later, when the child's appearance revealed her black heritage, welfare took her away from the Joneses and put her in a foster home. Mr. and Mrs. Jones battled in the courts for five months to get her back and then gave up. "We have talked about appealing this, but the case probably would have taken years," Jones said. "By then the child would be several years old, and such a long court fight couldn't do her or us any good." During the court fight, the Joneses received a number of anonymous phone calls, harrassing them for wanting to adopt the black child.[11]

> Tommy's white mother was put in a state hospital in Michigan in 1961 by her husband, William Smith, after she suffered severe brain damage in a car accident. In 1966 Tommy was born, and hospital officials speculated that Tommy's father was a black patient. The hospital officials gave Tommy to William Smith by then divorced and remarried. When Smith attempted to have his divorce decree from his first wife altered to give him legal custody of Tommy, a four year legal battle began. Two lower courts ruled against the Smiths before an appeals court ruled in their favor. Race was the issue; no one questioned the Smith's ability to parent their other four children.[12]

> A white couple which an agency had approved as an adoptive home are not being permitted to adopt a black foster child which has been living in their home for over a year. The white couple had cooperated with the birth mother in arranging visits, as long as the birth mother had said she would eventually take her baby back. It was after the baby was relinquished for adoption that the foster parents made their request for adoption and were turned down by the agency. The couple has chosen to remain anonymous while the internal appeals procedure goes forth.[13]

> Richard and Joan Daniels, a white couple from Georgia, are appealing their case all the way to the U.S. Supreme Court. The Daniels were given John as a foster child in December 1973 when he was 29 days old. By the time John was four months old his black heritage began to show. A doctor decided John was definitely of mixed race. That did not matter to the Daniels; when his mother relinquished him, they wanted to adopt him. "Why, John is our *family*!" Joan declared impatiently. The agency disagreed, and in May 1976 John was taken from the Daniels.

---

[a]All names have been changed to maintain the anonymity of the parties involved.

With the help of the American Civil Liberties Union, the Daniels are fighting to get him back.[14]

The story of the Smiths with the child born in a state hospital is quite unusual. The other stories illustrate the two most common instances in which white families acquire black children and then lose them: One, when the white birth mother has either lied about or been unaware of the race of the father, so that the agency does not know the baby's racial background until a few months after birth; and two, when white foster parents are given a black child to whom they become attached (when the child later becomes available for adoption, the white parents are refused).

Why Whites Adopt Black Children

Not all white foster parents who ask to adopt their black foster child have been refused. A number have adopted.[15] And it is the motivation of foster parents that is the easiest to understand. They already have the child and have grown to love her or him. But what about other whites, those who apply to adopt a black child whom they have never seen? Given the potential for discrimination and the low status and negative attitudes toward blacks, why would a white family want to adopt a black child?[16]

From her interviews with over a hundred whites who have adopted black children, Joyce Ladner answers:

> Many of these parents have a commitment to the goals of an integrated society whereby individuals are judged on their own merit instead of being evaluated on their racial group membership. Their commitment is also to justice, equality, understanding, and acceptance of all people, without regard for their racial, cultural, religious, or other background.[17]

When living with a black brother or sister, the parents also expect that their white biological children will have a strong sense of racial justice. The parents maintain that it is quite acceptable to view adoption as a social contribution as long as this is not the primary motivating force.

The earliest known adoptions of black children by whites occurred in the late 1940s and early 1950s. But these were very few. The minor boom of interracial adoptions involving black children did not begin until the late 1960s.[18] (See table 6-1.) It was the civil rights movement that made it possible for small numbers of whites to do what would have been almost unthinkable a few years earlier.

The adoption of a black child has been an overlay on the couple's basic desire to have a child and to get the child through adoption. A significant

Table 6-1
Black Children Adopted by Whites, as Reported in Opportunity Surveys, 1968–1976

Year	Placements of Black Children with Whites	Number of Agencies Reporting
1968	733	194
1969	1447	345
1970	2284	427
1971	2574	468
1972	1569	461
1973	1091	434
1974	747	458
1975	831[a]	565
1976	1070[b]	575

Source: Opportunity's annual national surveys of adoption agencies, 1968–1976. Opportunity is located at 2301 N.W. Glisan Street, Portland, Oregon 97210.

[a]This figure reflects an increase in the number of agencies reporting; when reports from the same agencies are compared, there is a decline between 1974 and 1975.

[b]Preliminary data.

minority of the whites who ultimately adopted a black child wanted to adopt because they could not have a child.[19] Others were motivated by a concern for overpopulation and, while being able to conceive and bear a child, chose not to do so. Smaller numbers undoubtedly were concerned about genetic diseases or the mother's health during a pregnancy, or they simply did not want to risk getting yet another child of the same sex.

Having social support also helped parents adopt across racial lines. Of 125 whites who adopted in the 1950s and 1960s, about one-tenth reported that before they adopted they knew someone else who had adopted a child of another race.[20] In another study, involving whites who had adopted black, Korean, and American Indian children in a somewhat later period, almost half the adopting couples had known someone who had adopted a child of another race before they took the step themselves.[21] This is particularly remarkable when we realize that adoption across racial lines is a very rare occurrence.

One way the parents find one another is through adoptive parent organizations. Already by 1969 at least 47, and probably many more, such organizations were in existence.[22] Some of the organizations for parents adopting across racial lines had been formed in earlier years by white parents adopting American Indian, Korean, and other Asian children. Others, like the Open Door Society of Minnesota, begun in 1966, were formed by parents who had adopted black children.[23]

The various organizations' programs have included some attempt to encourage black adopters, and the organizations certainly have had no policy of racial exclusion. In fact, built on friendship networks of whites and focused mainly on the adoption problems of whites, the organizations' memberships have ended up almost entirely white and their greatest successes have involved the recruitment of other white adopters.[24]

The very early impetus for whites adopting black children came from the white adoptive applicants.[25] In the early 1960s in Minnesota, for example, agencies launched a campaign to attract black adopters for black children. Quite unexpectedly, from the point of view of the agencies, a few whites applied also. (Several black couples also applied, willing to accept a child of another race, but the black couples were encouraged to apply for black youngsters since so many black youngsters needed homes.)

Cautiously, a few Minnesota agencies began raising the possibility of adopting black children to other whites who applied.[26] What happened in Minnesota undoubtedly happened in other areas as well. For example, in a 1972-1973 study of 125 white families living in seven different metropolitan areas who had adopted black children, almost one-third of the families reported that the idea of adopting a black child was first suggested by someone else, usually an agency social worker.

Many of the parents acknowledged that they had less difficulty adopting a black child than they would have had in adopting a child with a serious physical handicap, a retarded child, or a child more than 7 years old—other categories of children who also needed adoptive homes during this period. For a little over one-tenth of the families, the decision to adopt a black child was made after learning that black children were the only children available for adoption.[27]

Thus, the motives of the white parents who have adopted minority children are a combination of idealism, self-interest, and an honest appraisal of what they feel they can handle. The main satisfactions the parents derive from the adoptions are the satisfactions which any parent could be expected to have (table 6-2).

Agencies and Transracial Adoption

Since the avoidance of risk plays such an important role in decision making in adoptions, one wonders how adoption agencies ever could have gotten involved in anything as extraordinary as placing black children with white families.
Part of the answer has been suggested above: here and there white families expressed an interest, and here and there a few agencies, out of their oversupply of black children, obliged.

The black children the agencies gave out were almost always children who had had one white birth parent. My speculation is that the white parent was

Table 6-2

White Parents[a] with Black Children Reporting Particular Benefits from Having Adopted, Seven Metropolitan Areas, 1972-1973

Possible Benefit	Percentage Reporting Benefit Very Much or Much
Has given me a great deal of satisfying companionship	77
Has enabled me to express the deep love for children I have always had	69
Has enabled me to give a home to a child whom nobody seemed to want	54
Has made my marriage richer	49
Has made me feel more like a whole person	36
Has made me feel that I'm doing something toward furthering the cause of an integrated society	35
Has brought my spouse and me closer together	28
Has prevented me from becoming too selfish, too self-centered	27
Has made me feel that I am helping to compensate for the inequities of our society	23
Has made me feel proud about being able to make a contribution to the community	23
Has made me feel less lonely	22
Has enabled me to fulfill my duty to have a family	18

Source: Adapted from Lucille J. Grow and Deborah Shapiro, *Black Children, White Parents: A Study of Transracial Adoption* (New York: Child Welfare League of America, 1974), p. 83, table 3-5.

[a]Parents of 125 children.

usually the mother. Even when an agency already had several black children waiting for adoptive homes, agency personnel would find it difficult to refuse a relinquishment request from a white mother about to have a child fathered by a black man. A white mother with an illegitimate black child could be expected to have a very difficult time in the white community. As was pointed out in chapter 1, agencies refusing to accept relinquishment on the children of black women was common. Even when the father was white, the mother was black, and her baby was black, it would have been assumed that the black unwed mother and her black baby would be accepted by the black community.

Anecdotal material supports my speculation on the race of the mothers of the biracial children given out by adoption agencies. Often articles about black children adopted by whites mention the child's white biological mother.[28]

Before black-appearing black children were placed with white families, it was accepted practice for white-appearing black children to be placed with white families. In the 1950s the advice of the Child Welfare League of America, the national standard-setting organization in adoption, was that agencies place children of interracial background who appeared to be white in white families.[29] Agencies were encouraged to consult geneticists or anthropologists in questionable cases. Such consultation was necessary because in American society a person who has any Negroid racial traits at all is defined as black.

When a child is under 6 months old, it is difficult to correctly predict the child's adult appearance from a racial point of view. From time to time mistakes were made, and a child who later appeared to be black would be placed in a white home. At other times a white mother would lie about the race of the father of her child. In such cases, too, black children were placed in white homes.

Sometimes the adopting parents would reject the black-appearing child and bring him or her back to the agency; at other times the parents would accept and keep the child. If the adoption had not been finalized, some agencies probably took black-appearing children away from the parents, regardless of the parents' wishes; other agencies probably let the parents who desired to keep their child do so. In those cases where both the parents and the agency permitted the adoption to continue, the agencies, by accident, had been involved in the placement of a black child with a white family.

In the 1950s, there were few interracial babies coming to adoption agencies. For example, over a 14-year period beginning in 1947, the Dight Institute for Human Genetics of the University of Minnesota had only 26 inquiries about black-white children from adoption agencies.[30] As interracial dating became more common in the 1960s, interracial babies became more common also.

In the 1960s, agencies were not finding black homes for all the black children in their care; the interracial babies who appeared to have some black ancestry were not getting homes either. Since some workers already had placed black-appearing children in white homes by accident, one can see how these workers would be tempted to honor the requests of the few white couples who expressed a desire to adopt black children.

After a few such transracial placements worked out, one can see also how social workers would be tempted to begin suggesting such an alternative to other white couples who applied. In the 1960s, under the influence of the civil rights movement, some white couples began to make such requests, and a few social workers began to make such suggestions to their other white clients.

Throughout the 1958-1972 period, the Child Welfare League of America (CWLA) standards for adoption service included the following statement:

Racial background in itself should not determine the selection of the home for a child. It should not be assumed (by the agency or staff members) that difficulties will necessarily arise if adoptive parents and children are of different racial origin.

In 1958, a qualifying statement cautioned that children with the same racial characteristics as their adopting parents could more easily become integrated into the average family. In 1963 the qualifying statement was deleted, probably in response to the growing number of successful placements of Korean and American Indian children being made with white Americans. But those writing the standards must have been aware that the standards applied to blacks as well.

By 1968 a qualifying statement cautiously encouraged transracial adoption.

In most communities there are families who have the capacity to adopt a child whose racial background is different from their own. Such couples should be encouraged to consider such a child.[31]

The whites interested in adopting black children have been very well qualified by conventional adoption criteria. The studies have been small, but the findings have been fairly consistent. The white adopters of black children have been well-off, educated people, often professionals. Frequently the mothers did not work. Some evidence even suggests that the whites who adopt black children are better off financially than whites who adopt white children.[32]

In the early 1970s, the agencies and social workers involved in placing black children with white families were seen in two ways. From one point of view, the social workers were to be praised: they were showing a concern about black children when most of the social work profession was not. They were courageously braking the American taboo against interracial families.

From another point of view, the social workers were just continuing with adoption business as usual, avoiding the black community. The social workers making such placements worked with a familiar type of client and followed their usual procedures. No effort was being made to recruit black adopters or to overcome the communication problems of working with black clients.[33]

Many black social workers and some white social workers took this latter view:

I suggest that the myth of "no black homes available" is a social agency cop-out for not devising innovative and creative ways of facing up to the problem—a perfect example of "benign neglect."[34]

Black families are not available for black children because most agencies are not actively recruiting black families.[35]

Virtually all the people on the boards and staffs of adoption agencies
are white. They do not involve black people in policy formulation or in
day-to-day programming. They do not know the black community;
they insist on doing "business as usual" and then are surprised when
they cannot recruit black families for adoption. They do not reach the
black community because they do not know it.[36]

White social workers feel more comfortable with white couples, and
thus see transracial adoption as the easiest way to place black children.[37]

The problems black clients have in adopting have been well documented in earlier
chapters.

The black social workers were also very concerned about the healthy psychological development of the black children adopted by whites. In 1972 the National Association of Black Social Workers took this position:

Black children should be placed only with Black families whether in
foster care or for adoption. Black children belong physically, psychologically and culturally in Black families in order that they receive the
total sense of themselves and develop a sound projection of their future.
Human beings are products of their environment and develop their
sense of values, attitudes, and self-concept within their own family
structures. Black children in white homes are cut off from the healthy
development of themselves as Black people.[38]

In 1973, in response to the stand taken by the National Association of Black
Social Workers, the Child Welfare League of America completely changed its
standards on race. The standards now read: "It is preferable to place childen in
families of their own racial background." The explanatory material points out
that "children placed in adoptive families with similar racial characteristics can
become more easily integrated into the average family group and community."
Agencies are urged to use local and national adoption exchanges before settling
for a family of another race.[39]

By 1978 the National Association of Black Social Workers was no longer
supporting the notion that black foster homes were better than white adoptive
homes. However, they maintained their original opposition to whites adopting
black children.

We stand firmly on the conviction that a white home is not a suitable
placement for Black children and contend it is totally unnecessary.[40]

Although it is not a major element in their position and is not written down
in any of their literature, several black social workers, in conversation, have
mentioned what they see as a double standard: whites are adopting black children, but blacks are not adopting white children. The obvious explanation is

that black children are in oversupply and white children are not. True, but circumstances could arise in which black parents would be the preferred candidates to adopt a white child—except for their race. For example, a black foster parent could be raising a white child and once the child was freed for adoption, wish to adopt him or her. A black couple could be given a "black" baby who later appeared to be white; already attached to the baby, the black couple could still want to adopt her or him. Just as there are whites who want to adopt a child who needs a home regardless of race, so there are also blacks who feel the same way and who would be willing to adopt a white, hard-to-place child.

In 1955 a district court prevented a black man from adopting his white wife's white, out-of-wedlock child. The whereabouts of the white birth father were unknown. An appeals court finally approved the adoption, but the fact that the case had to go to court at all illustrates the double standard some black social workers have mentioned.[41] A South Carolina law which is still on the books makes the double standard explicit: it is legal for whites to adopt black children; it is not legal for blacks to adopt white children.[42]

In all my research on adoption, I have come across references to only four agency placements of white children with black families.[43]

The opposition to whites adopting black children has had an impact. Adoptions in all groups have declined, but the decline has been greatest in the adoption of black children by whites (table 6-3). (For a discussion of the impact of abortion on adoption, see chapter 1.)

One group hit by the change in practice is the whites who have adopted one black child and would like to adopt another. The families strongly prefer that their child not be the only black member of the family, but some have not been able to find agencies in their area willing to place a second black child with them. (It is not a question of their parenting ability; agencies are willing to place children from other racial groups with them.[44])

Regardless of their attempts to adopt additional children, almost all whites who have adopted black children are aware of the National Association of Black Social Workers' position that whites cannot raise black children well. Some have been dismayed and hurt; others, angry; still others, untouched. A few have even agreed, opposing most transracial placements on grounds similar to those expressed by the National Association of Black Social Workers.[45]

Although differing on transracial adoption, the white adoptive parents' groups do have something in common with the black social workers' organization. Both are engaged in a serious critique of the way adoption is run in the United States. Both are concerned that agencies screen out qualified adopters and ignore children who need homes.[46]

Outside the social work profession, black organizations have not taken an active stand against whites adopting black children.[47] One is tempted to speculate that this is because the other black groups, when they pause to think about

Table 6-3
Adoption Trends, 1969–1975

| | Percentage Change in Adoption[a] | | | | |
| | Black Children | | | White Children | Number of Agencies Reporting |
	All Homes	Black Homes	White Homes	All Homes	
1969 to 1970	37	23	70	b	252
1970 to 1971	4	5	4	b	252
1971 to 1972	−20	−10	−39	b	252
1972 to 1973	−18	−14	−29	−15	345
1973 to 1974	−10	−7	−20	−6	271
1974 to 1975	−1	1	−11	8	319

Source: Opportunity's annual national surveys of adoption agencies, 1968-1975.

[a]The percent change is reported only for agencies for which reports were received in both years.

[b]Not available.

transracial adoption at all, see it in broad historical terms and interpret whites adopting black children as a hopeful sign of change in racist white America.

Although other black groups have not had questions about whites adopting black children, black individuals have, wondering at least if the white couples knew what they were getting into: "Do you know that this is going to pose all kinds of visible and invisible problems? Do you realize how 'freaky' some people will think you are; and how others will call you dogooders?"

Opposition from Relatives and Friends

White couples have experienced opposition from other quarters, too, including their own relatives. In a study of 125 whites who had adopted black children, Grow and Shapiro found that more than half the parents reported that all their relatives supported them right from the beginning. Other relatives came around after the adoption, so that only about 15 percent of the relatives remained opposed to the adoption. According to the parents, the relatives were opposed not to the idea of adoption, but specifically to the child's racial background.[49]

A study by Simon and Altstein, of 200 white families with at least one nonwhite child, found less than one-third of the grandparents, aunts, and uncles approved right from the start. Slightly over one-third were disapproving at first but eventually came to friendly terms with the adopting families. Almost 40 percent continued to reject the adopted child. When there was some degree of reconciliation after the adoption, sometimes limits were put on the relationship. For example, the adopting parents would not visit in the grandparents' home; or if they visited there, they would not sleep overnight. None of the parents in this study reported accepting a compromise where the grandparents were permitted to have a relationship with the natural grandchildren and not the adopted grandchildren.

While accepting their grandchild, some grandparents nonetheless clung to their stereotypes and viewed their grandchild as different from other blacks. A small number continued to refer to blacks as "niggers."[50] Opposition from relatives on racial grounds was found in another study also.[51]

Falk found that when friends, neighbors, and relatives were ranked according to their degree of approval of transracial adoption (the adoption of a black child by white parents), friends were the most approving, relatives next, and neighbors least approving. In their study of 200 families, Simon and Altstein found only one couple where the adoption of a black child cost the new parents the friendship of a couple they had considered their best friends. Ladner suggests that friends are more approving than relatives because people choose as their friends persons with whom they have much in common.[52]

Ladner is the only researcher thus far who has explored the reactions of black friends, in particular, to whites adopting black children. She found that the reactions of black friends were not uniform. Some were very supportive; others expressed strong opposition.[53]

Opposition from Neighbors and Strangers

The troubles the families have experienced have ranged from just unpleasant to frightening and dangerous.

> One family reported that after they brought their black child home they received an ultimatum from the City Council ording them to leave town. The family called the FBI for protection. They continued to live where they had been and, although their relationship with neighbors and others is not friendly, they and their children have not been the victims of insults or violence.[54]

> One woman was taunted as a "nigger lover"— and worse. "It drives me right up the wall," she says. "It's frightening to think anyone in this neighborhood could feel threatened by seeing a little boy run past the house."[55]

> Living in a neighborhood that excluded black families, a couple reported

that the family next door did not speak to them after they adopted; other families forbid their children to play with any of the adopting family's children. Black children were not permitted to swim in the neighborhood pool.[56]

In Los Angeles in 1966 racist neighbors threw garbage on the lawn and wrote "Watts" on the door of a white family that adopted a black child. As a result of these and other harassments, the family made the painful decision to send the child back to the adoption agency.[57]

Simon and Altstein report that few of the adopting parents in their study— less than 10 percent—had trouble with friends or neighbors about the adoption.[58]

Somewhere the experiences with neighbors and acquaintances meld into the experiences with strangers. Falk reports that about 10 percent of the couples who adopted black children had been subjected to insulting remarks and phone calls.[59] Ladner found that most families in her study had had unpleasant experiences with white strangers. The families were frequently the objects of curiosity as people stared relentlessly at their unusual-looking family. Some couples had not been prepared to undergo the stares and curiosity, sometimes well meaning, which they received. In fact, two couples of Ladner's sample of 135 said they probably would not have adopted had they known they would be stared at so.[60]

The prejudice that follows the transracial adopters into their families and neighborhoods and on the street can affect them in their employment as well. For example, if working for a large corporation, a family member may lose eligibility for a transfer or promotion because he or she would be socially ostracized or unacceptable in the new environment.[61] And what happens when business needs require membership in an all-white country club? The *New York Times* reported speculation that the pastor of the Plains Baptist Church of Plains, Georgia, resigned because of disapproval by some church members of the Slater family's adoption of a child who was not white.[62]

The white couples who adopt black children often have other children whom they have produced. These white children can also be affected by the animosity of white society toward blacks. As Ladner points out, there are many occasions for the white siblings to defend themselves and their black brother or sister from their playmates' cruel insults. One couple mentioned that their children were confused by all the stares and questions from strangers because of the couple's two adopted daughters.[63] A daughter once commented to her babysitter, "I don't know why people have to ask if he's my real brother, just because his skin is different."[64]

Parents Fight Back

Whether the rejection is from grandparents or other relatives, friends, neighbors, or strangers, discrimination and rejection visited on the white families of black children carry over to the black children themselves. Parents have reported ways they have tried to defend and protect their children.

> One mother observed, "Some people, since our child is black-white, try to ignore the fact that he is black. We simply remind them."

> The parent of a three-year-old reported, "At one point a lady approached our family, pointed to our very special son and said, 'What's that?' " I answered, "Why that is a little boy!" and walked on.

> One family attempted to show their four-year-old black child that she is healthy whereas society is not because it is sick with racism.

> After their children had told them of being "put down" because of being the bi-racial children of white parents, the parents carefully reviewed "the reality of their biological parentage (half and half), of their adoptive parents (white), and of some of the 'sickness' in our society."

> The parents of a three-year-old black child interpret the comments of the critical or curious about their daughter's features or hair when she is present by turning such comments into "compliments about how pretty this aspect of her is, how nice differences among people are."[65]

Sometimes the discriminatory behavior can appear friendly.

> "Teachers bend over backward to be nice. It may not be a negative form of prejudice but it is still relating color to your actions."

> ". . . one friend 'goes out of her way' to praise the beauty and intelligence of our two black children."[66]

> "I had to bear down extra hard on Jerry," relates one father whose 9-year-old black son has older white brothers. "Jerry gets so much attention that he tends to regard himself as special—above the rules." Jerry's teachers had let him get by "until he figured all he had to do was smile and it wouldn't matter if he hadn't done his homework." It took a couple of emphatic meetings with school authorities before Jerry began to receive equal treatment.[67]

Black Acceptance

Basically the incidents of rejection which have been described are the negative reactions of whites. From her discussions with white parents, Ladner reports that the parents felt that ordinary black strangers were not hostile to them.[68]

Survey results also support the notion that blacks are much more accepting than whites of interracial families of various sorts. For example, a 1972 Gallup

poll showed that nearly 60 percent of blacks and only 25 percent of whites
approved of black-white marriages. And in earlier years, whites had been even
less approving. In 1958, only 4 percent of whites had approved of interracial
marriages.[69]

No survey has been done of white attitudes toward whites adopting black
children. A survey of 150 blacks in Dayton, Ohio, in 1971 revealed that 80 percent of those interviewed preferred adoption by a white family to keeping a
black child in a foster home or institution. About 80 percent of those interviewed also felt that "liberal white parents would be qualified to raise a black
child, if they (the white parents) gave up some of their white culture in order
to give the child a chance to develop some black identity."[70]

Black Children in a White World

Ironically, although the black community appears to be more accepting of
interracial families, every study of the white families who have adopted black
children has shown that 80 to 90 percent have chosen to live in all-white or
predominantly white neighborhoods.[71]

In some cases, the white parents in interracial families have been quite
aware of the negative attitudes of their neighbors toward blacks. One-third
of the 125 families interviewed in Grow and Shapiro's study thought that their
neighbors would disapprove if black families moved into the neighborhood. It
is noteworthy that the families whom Grow and Shapiro interviewed lived in
Boston, Chicago, Los Angeles, Detroit, Minneapolis, Seattle, and Montreal—
large metropolitan areas where presumably some integrated neighborhoods
existed.[72]

Like their neighborhoods, the black children's schools tended to be white
also. At the time of Grow and Shapiro's study, only two of the children had
black teachers and only one-tenth of the children had had a black teacher at
any time during their schooling. The children had few black classmates as
well.[73]

About 80 percent of the white parents in Grow and Shapiro's study reported having black friends or acquaintances. About 60 percent of the parents
reported socializing with black friends or acquaintances in one another's
homes.[74] Once invited to the parents' home, the black friends could become
acquainted with the black children and perhaps serve as role models for them.

It is possible that many of the black children whose parents did not invite
blacks into their homes lived in totally white worlds in their neighborhood,
school, and family. Grow and Shapiro do not present their data in such a way
that it is possible to find out. Anecdotal accounts of such families do exist.
For example, Ladner reports a white adopting couple with no black friends
and no intention of making any. The white couple are not hostile toward

blacks, Ladner explains; it is just that they have always lived in an almost completely segregated world.[75] Jones reports a white couple adopting a black 6-year-old where neither parent had ever had any contact with a black woman who was in any role other than a domestic or salesperson.[76] One white mother saw nothing wrong in her black daughter having all white playmates except for a young black boy whom the daughter sees when the boy's parents come to visit. "After all, June is not all black anyway," the mother explained.[77]

Segregation into a white world may make it difficult for the black child to relate to other blacks.

> A 2-year-old cried whenever a darkskinned person approached him. The mother tried to reassure the social worker: "You don't have to worry about it because I doubt he'll ever live near black people. I know he won't as long as he is growing up." The child himself was dark brown skinned.[78]

> A black teenager raised by whites hated blacks, even though her closest friends had been black.

> A black teenager found it necessary to lock herself in her own room to learn the black dialect in order to belong.[79]

A surprising number of white parents were unconcerned about their black child's future ability to relate to other blacks. In Grow and Shapiro's study, one-third of the fathers and one-fourth of the mothers were uncertain about or disagreed with the statement that "Black children adopted by white families should be helped to acquire a feeling of identity with the black community."[80]

Being surrounded by whites may become more of a problem as the black youngsters, now mainly preschoolers and elementary school students, reach dating age. Although the adopting parents generally do not object to transracial dating and marriage, their neighbors may well object.[81] In fact, many of the parents anticipate this problem. They expect rejection to be particularly strong from the white parents of their black adolescents' white friends. Overwhelmingly, however, the adopting parents believe that their children's upbringing will help them get through the crisis.[82]

Parent Attitudes and Healthy Child Development

It is precisely the children's upbringing that is at issue. It would be ideal to have a comparison between black children adopted by black parents and black children adopted by white parents, but no such comparison is available. What is possible is a comparison of the adjustments of black children living with white parents with different kinds of characteristics. One would expect that an important factor in a black child's adjustment in a white family would be the parents' acceptance of the child as a black person. Using Grow and Shapiro's data, we find exactly that.

Adopted black children thought to be obviously black by their parents are more likely to be doing better in terms of a composite adjustment score developed by Grow and Shapiro than black children whose white parents do not think they are obviously black.

Similarly, adopted black children whose white parents think they are obviously black are less likely to have psychosomatic ailments such as colds, headaches, and tiredness than adopted black children whose white parents do not think they are obviously black.[83] The findings are more striking when we realize that children given the same general description by interviewers are called obviously black by some parents and not by others (table 6-4).

Grow and Shapiro asked parents to report whether their child had experienced some sort of cruelty. Half reported that their child had been subject to some type of cruelty, usually name calling or heckling and occasionally physical abuse. One-third of the parents reported no cruelty at all, and about one-fifth reported that no such problem could arise because the child's peers did not know about her or his racial background.[84]

One might expect that children who have experienced cruelty would be

Table 6-4
Interviewer's Description of Child's Appearance, by Parents' Perception of Child's Appearance, Seven Metropolitan Areas, 1972-1973

| Interviewer's Description of Child's Appearance | Total Number | *Parent's Perception of Child's Appearance* | | |
| | | *Percentage* | | |
		Total	Obviously Black	Not Obviously Black
No Negroid features				
Fair	19	100	5	95
Light brown	25	100	48	52
Negroid features				
Fair	12	100	17	83
Light brown	45	100	80	20
Dark brown	12	100	92	8
Total	113	100	55	45

Source: Adapted from Lucille J. Grow and Deborah Shapiro, *Black Children, White Parents: A Study of Transracial Adoption* (New York: Child Welfare League of America, 1974), p. 110.

less well adjusted than children who have not. Paradoxically, Grow and Shapiro's data suggest that the opposite is the case.

> Children whose parents report that their children have experienced cruelty have fewer problems in relationships with other children than children whose parents report their children have experienced no cruelty.
>
> Children whose parents report that their child has experienced cruelty are less likely to have psychosomatic symptoms such as frequent colds, headaches or a feeling of tiredness, than children whose parents report that their children have experienced no cruelty.[85]

How can this paradox be resolved? The median age of the children in Grow and Shapiro's study was almost 9. It seems likely that, in fact, all the children who appeared black had experienced some kind of cruelty. If that is true, then Grow and Shapiro asked parents whether their children had experienced cruelty, what Grow and Shapiro learned about was the quality of the communication between the children and their parents on racial issues.

If the parent was understanding of racial problems, then presumably the child could turn to the parent for comfort and advice when an incident occurred. If the parent was overwhelmed by guilt or whatever and sent out signals that he or she did not want to hear about racial problems, the child would quickly learn not to share such incidents. Left without parental advice and support, the child would develop problems, either striking out at peers or turning the anger inward on himself or herself and subsequently developing physical symptoms.

The white parents who accept the fact that their black children face racial discrimination and struggle to help them deal with it are teaching their children survival skills. The white parents are probably not as knowledgeable in this area as black parents, who have dealt with discrimination all their lives; but the white parents can offer their black children some help. The white parents who deny racial discrimination by not discussing it or by pretending that oppression is universal are offering their black children little help in the present and laying the groundwork for problems in the future.

Of particular concern in this regard are the parents who have not even told their black children about their black heritage. In Grow and Shapiro's study, where the average age of the children was 9 years, 8 of the 114 families still had not told their children about their black heritage.[86]

Black Heritage

A parent's main way to help a child value herself or himself is through loving appreciation, but an understanding of black culture and history is important too. The white parents realized this. In Grow and Shapiro's study, 93 percent of the white mothers and 86 percent of the white fathers agreed that it is very important for a black child to develop pride in her or his black heritage. Given their white social worlds, the most common way white parents helped their black children appreciate their black heritage was through written materials.

Of the families in Grow and Shapiro's study, 85 percent reported having read or having in their homes books written by or about blacks. Almost one-third reported trips to museums and special black cultural events.[87] Three-fourths of the white parents in Simon and Altstein's study said they were trying to teach their children about the children's own racial groups using books, pictures, toys, and music.[88]

The studies make no effort to assess how extensive or shallow is the parents' understanding of any of the materials used. Jones, aware that a number of white parents know so little of black culture, is concerned that the white parents focus simply on music and dancing and neglect other aspects.[89]

Even the well-intentioned parent can make mistakes. For example, one couple told Ladner how they read a story about a black hero to their black daughter every night and read a regular fairytale to their white children.[90] One hopes that soon the parents will realize that they can read stories about black heroes to their white children and fairytales to their black child.

Parental Prejudices and Growth

Having parents free of racial stereotypes is also important. As illustrated below, some white parents still have quite a way to go in this regard:

> I think black people have a certain self-destructive elment in their culture. . . .
>
> About their adopted son: "Mel Jr. has a lot of rhythm." About their adopted daughter: "I want her to dress pretty like the colored girls dress when she gets to be a teenager, and not dowdy like the white girls. . . ."
>
> A child's skin turned very dark, and the family minimized his contacts with the outside world by seldom taking him along when they went out.[91]

Little evidence is available on how rare or common such views and behavior are.

Being a parent is a continuing role, not one over in a few hours or a day. And as their black children are growing, some of the white parents are growing also. Parenting a black child forces the white parents to analyze their own feelings and attitudes on a variety of issues, including race.[92] Of the parents in Simon and Altstein's study, 63 percent claimed that some change had occurred in their attitudes and beliefs since adoption. Most felt "they had become more racially and socially sensitive." They felt that they had become more aware of manifestations of prejudice, and they believed more strongly than before in the importance of treating people alike and not emphasizing distinctions that stemmed from racial characteristics.[93]

In 1970 one white mother reported her and her husband's growing consciousness.

> My son said, "I can't play at that neighbor's house. They don't like Negroes." This experience jarred us to recognize that the very nature of our society would someday force him to find his primary identity with the Black race. If we never mentioned his color, he could very well come to feel that we were ashamed of it. Thus to help give him a sense of security and pride in his race, we no longer ignored his blackness; we began teaching him of its beauty.

> Our son saw on television the dogs and water hoses and faces contorted with high-pitched prejudice. Then Martin Luther King, Jr., was assassinated. My husband and I came to see that we could never fulfill our obligation to John unless we ourselves bridged across the racial gap to identify meaningfully with the black people.

> After escaping death in a serious car accident, we decided to go all the way with this thing. By this time we have entered deeply into a world which to us was once forbidden and strange: the world of the black ghetto. There we have developed deep and meaningful friendships with wonderful people.

> John has really taken to his black identity. Every summer he and his dad have a contest to see who can get the darkest. A black woman gives me insights into matters of personal attention such as hair care, with which white people have had no experience. John is so sold on the greatness of his race that he convinced kids in his class to write "Black is beautiful" on their tennis shoes.

> When people rave about what sacrifices we are making to have this poor little boy in our home, I get shook and embarrassed. They are reading it all wrong. John has brought us a wealth of blessings.

> He has opened to us doors to an unbelievable world with a rich culture and a truly great people. Experiences of identifying with deep need and sharing imminent danger have so bonded friendships that our whole family has grown in understanding what life is all about.[94]

A person critical of whites adopting black children might ask what happens to the youngsters who do not have parents willing to grow? And what happens to the black children whose parents grow too slowly?

Dolls and Black Identity

The question of the development of a positive black identity in black children
living in white families has been explored directly with the children involved by
using a technique originally developed in the 1930s by Kenneth and Mamie
Clark. The technique uses dolls to examine a child's racial preferences, awareness, and identity. The work was done by Simon and Altstein and involved
120 black adopted children and their 209 white sisters and brothers.

Using brown and white dolls, the children in Simon and Altstein's study
were asked to point to the doll that "looks like you." The white children and
the black children were equally accurate in identifying their own race. Again
using the dolls, the children were asked to point to the doll that (1) looks like
a colored child, (2) looks like a black child, (3) looks like a white child. Selec-
tions of dolls were used as a measure of racial awareness. There was no
evidence of a difference in racial awareness between white and black children.

Finally, the children were asked to point to the doll that (1) you would like
to play with best, (2) is a nice doll, (3) looks bad, (4) is a nice color. Again,
there was no evidence of differences between black children and white children;
the children favored black dolls and white dolls about equally. This study, done
in the early 1970s, is the first study of racial attitudes and identity among young
children in American society that has not found a racial preference for whites
among both black children and white children.

Earlier studies involving children raised in families of their own race, including one done as late as 1968, had shown white racial preferences on the part of
both black children and white children.[95] A subsequent study, a small one done
by Womack involving black children in the Seattle area, suggests that the racial
preferences of black children raised by black parents have improved. In Womack's
study, the black children living with black parents showed no preference for
whites; the black children living with white parents also showed no racial preference for whites.[96] Altogether, the work by Simon and Altstein and by Womack
suggests that the whites who have adopted black children have been able to raise
their children to know their own racial group and appreciate it.

Overall Adjustment

In their study of black children adopted by whites, Grow and Shapiro used a
variety of measures of adoption success, including some tests on the children
themselves. From these various measures, Grow and Shapiro developed an
overall score of adjustment. By using this score as a guide, 96 of 125 of the
adoptions were judged to be doing quite well—a success rate of 77 percent.
According to Grown and Shapiro, the success rate of 77 percent compares favorably with the success rate of other adoption studies, including studies of white
infants adopted by whites.

Of 29 adoptions in trouble, there was evidence that in 16 the racial difference between the child and her or his parents was a contributing factor to the
problem.[97]

All the children in Grow and Shapiro's study were at least 6 years old and
had been in their adoptive homes at least three years. In fact, most of the
youngsters had been with their white families longer, seven years on the average.

IQ Scores

In the early 1970s Sandra Scarr and Richard A. Weinberg of the University of
Minnesota did IQ tests on 130 black children 4 years of age and older who had
been adopted by whites and were living in Minnesota. Their dramatic finding is
that these adopted black youngsters had an average IQ of 106, one standard
deviation or 15 full points above the average IQ of 90 usually achieved by black
children living in the North Central region and reared in the homes of their birth.
The 99 youngsters adopted at an early age scored even higher, about 110 on the
average.[98]

Twenty-eight black children adopted by whites and living in the Seattle
area were tested by another researcher, William Womack, who reports that the
black youngsters in his study had an average IQ of 115.[99]

The scores of the black youngsters in both studies compare favorably with
the average score of 113 reported by Leahy for white children adopted by professional families.[100]

The IQ scores of the black youngsters had obviously been influenced by
their adopted family environments which were culturally relevant to the tests,
yet another illustration of the cultural bias of IQ tests. The research makes
another important point as well; at least as far as an ability to learn from the
environment and to put that learning to work on a conventional IQ test, the
black youngsters adopted by whites have not been handicapped!

Summary

This chapter has seemed full of contradictory evidence. On the one hand, one
can find instance after instance of white parents having difficulty coping with
raising their black children. On the other, the parents generally feel quite positive about the adoptions themselves, and about 90 percent are willing to recommend adopting across racial lines to both black and white parents.[101] Ladner
reports that the psychiatrists interviewed for her study felt it was possible for
some white parents to rear emotionally healthy black children.[102] The various
studies on IQ, overall adjustment, and identity and self-concept all suggest that
the adopted children are doing quite well. Perhaps the answer is that most

parents make mistakes some of the time but only a few are making mistakes so much of the time that it is damaging to their children.

The studies examined in this chapter are small—not one involved as many as 150 black adopted youngsters. Perhaps larger studies would show different results. When the studies were done, the children were quite young. Whether and how the white parents meet their black children's developmental needs, time and further studies will have to tell.

In the meantime, the opposition of the National Association of Black Social Workers has had an impact. The Child Welfare League of America has changed the tone of its standards, discouraging placements across racial lines and encouraging agencies to recruit more black adoptive parents.[103]

Transracial placement goes against the American prejudice that people who are black and people who are white should not be part of the same family. Transracial placement goes against the traditional adoption practice of matching the adopted child as closely as possible with the adopting parents. Thus once opposition was raised, it is easy to see why the number of transracial adoptions being permitted was reduced.

At the height of the transracial adoption movement, one-third of all black children adopted were adopted by white families. By 1976 the figure had dropped to one-fourth.[104]

Through its various local chapters, the National Association of Black Social Workers has done quite a bit to encourage black adoptions. In New York City, for example, the NABSW's efforts have even resulted in the establishment of a counseling and referral service for black adoptive applicants.

The National Association of Black Social Workers and the Child Welfare League of America are right. More black adoptive homes *can* be found. Even the steps to take to find the black homes are known. Unfortunately, not enough agencies have been willing to take those steps.

There are blind spots on both sides in the debate on transracial adoption. Those who advocate transracial adoption tend to ignore the discrimination against would-be black adopters. Those who oppose whites adopting black children tend to ignore the thousands of black children who need permanent homes. With such thousands waiting, it is hard to see how even a spectacular recruitment effort could provide enough black homes. Since this is so, it is appropriate to consider the question of which whites, among those expressing an interest, ought to be permitted to adopt black children.

In an article by Morgenstern, Clayton Hagen, former adoption supervisor at Lutheran Social Service of Minnesota, takes the least restrictive position:

> "If an adoptive parent can make a child feel he's someone of value,
> and help him value others, that may be all the parent needs to worry
> about at the moment. If a child has a good concept of himself, he can
> meet all the problems we feel he'll encounter and not be overcome."[105] a

---

[a]Copyright 1971 by Newsweek, Inc. All rights reserved. Reprinted with permission.

Various other authorities have suggested some restrictions:

> Black caseworkers are almost essential to screen conscious and unconscious racial attitudes in white applicants.[106]

> Only those parents who are able to accept and live with differences should be allowed to adopt. Agencies should reject any would-be parent who engages in denial involving the child's color, hair texture, biological parentage, or any overt or latent characteristic.[107] (This includes those who insist a child is biracial and not black because socially the child would be black in the American context.)

> The applicants already have black friends.[108]

> The adoption of a black child should be the couple's first choice and not be regarded as second best when no white children are available.

> The family should live in an integrated neighborhood and be willing to send all their children to integrated schools. This would prevent the child from suffering the extra attention of being the lone black.

> The adoption should not be done to prove a point, such as to demonstrate independence from the parents' families, the couple's liberalism, or whatever.[109]

As flexible guidelines, the above suggestions should be quite helpful. But with or without guidelines, transracial adoption should not be permitted to take attention away from the major concern—to change the adoption situation so that more black people are able to become adoptive parents.

Notes

1. Estimated from statistics published for 1968 through 1976 by *Opportunity*, 2301 N.W. Glisan Street, Portland, Oregon 97210, and by the National Center for Social Statistics of the Department of Health, Education, and Welfare.

2. Joyce A. Ladner, *Mixed Families* (Garden City, N.Y.: Anchor Press, Doubleday, 1977), pp. 59, 149, 155, 159 copyright ©1977 by Joyce A. Ladner. Used by permission of Doubleday & Company, Inc. "Transracial Adoption" (Paper from the Adoption Bureau, Los Angeles).

3. James Hugh Johnston, *Race Relations in Virginia and Miscegenation in the South, 1776-1860* (Amherst: University of Massachusetts, 1970).

4. Maurice R. Davie, *Negroes in American Society* (New York: McGraw-Hill, 1949), p. 408. Albert I. Gordon, *Intermarriage* (Boston: Beacon Press, 1959), p. 222. Harr A. Ploski and Ernest Kaiser, eds., *Afro USA* (New York: Bellwether, 1971), p. 255.

5. My thanks to Carl Kessler for his careful search of all the state statutes.

6. Ga. Code Ann., § 74-410 (1973); and M.S.A. 8 27.3178 (545) (1962).

7. Code of S.C. Ann., § 16-17-460 (1977). The law is careful not to trample on established custom: "The provisions of this section shall not be construed so as to prevent the offices of a Negro in the family of any white person as a nurse."

8. Burns Ind. Stat. Ann., 31-3-1-2 (1977 p.p.); 10 Okla. St. Ann., § 60.12 (1966); and 1 P.S. § 331 and 333 (1978-79 p.p.). In the District of Columbia, an interracial couple challenged the court's requirement that race be put on the adoption petition, pointing out that this information was available to the court without putting it on the adoption petition itself. Furthermore, other factors relevant to the adoption placement also were not included on the petition. 307 A.2d 737 (D.C., 1973).

9. S.D.C.L., § 825-6-13 (1976).

10. K.R.S., § 199.471 (1977). The Kentucky law does require religious, ethic, and racial background to be taken into account if the natural parents request it.

11. *Washington Post* January 8, 1970. An Associated Press article dated January 7, 1970. Reprinted with permission.

12. "White Couple Wins Battle to Keep Boy," *Ann Arbor News* December 12, 1969, as published in *Adoptalk* March-April 1970, p. 3. Reprinted with permission from the Associated Press.

13. Editor's Note, *Adoptalk* January-March 1978, p. 2. Reprinted with permission.

14. Laughlin McDonald, "The Drummonds Want to Adopt a Racially Mixed Child Named Timmy," *Civil Liberties* May 1977, p. 4. Reprinted with permission. See also *Drummond v. Fulton Cty. Dept. of Family and Children Services,* 563 F.2d 1200 (C.A. 5, 1977). For another case see 311 N.E.2d 6 (Ohio, 1974).

15. Lucille J. Grow and Deborah Shapiro, *Black Children, White Parents: A Study of Transracial Adoption* (New York: Child Welfare League of America, 1974), p. 25.

16. Leon Chestang, "The Dilemma of Biracial Adoption," *Social Work* May 1972, p. 103.

17. Ladner, *Mixed Families,* pp. 92, 95f, 100.

18. Harriet Fricke, "Interracial Adoption: The Little Revolution," *Social Work* July 1965, p. 92. Joseph Morgenstern, "The New Face of Adoption," *Newsweek* September 13, 1971, p. 67. Rita James Simon and Howard Altstein, *Transracial Adoption* (New York: Wiley, 1977), p. 26.

19. Thomas E. Nutt and John A. Snyder, "Trans-Racial Adoption" (Report submitted to NIMH, February 1973); Simon and Altstein, *Transracial Adoption,* p. 83.

20. Grow and Shapiro, *Black Children, White Parents,* p. 69.

21. Simon and Altstein, *Transracial Adoption*, p. 95.

22. *Opportunity,* "Results of Survey of Interracial Adoption in the United States in 1968," June 1969, available from 2301 N.W. Glisan Street, Portland, Oregon 97210.

23. Sandra Scarr and Richard A. Weinberg, "IQ Performance of Black Children Adopted by White Families," *American Psychologist* October 1976, p. 727.

24. Barbara P. Griffin and Marvin S. Arffa, "Recruiting Adoptive Homes for Minority Children—One Approach," *Child Welfare* February 1970, pp. 105-107.

25. Ladner, *Mixed Families,* p. 62.

26. Fricke, "Interracial Adoption," p. 93.

27. Grow and Shapiro, *Black Children, White Parents,* pp. 69, 71, 75; and Simon and Altstein, *Transracial Adoption,* p. 86.

28. Little systematic evidence has been collected, but what does exist suggests that black children involved in transracial adoption usually have one white parent. Over a 12-year period, Gallay found that of 115 nonwhite children adopted by whites in Canada, 107 (92 percent) were part white. The majority had one white parent. In Grow and Shapiro's study, 103 of 118 black children adopted by whites had one white birth parent. All the first 35 black children placed by the L.A. County Bureau of Adoptions had one white parent.

In my 1970 survey of 207 adoption workers in the District of Columbia and Baltimore metropolitan areas, only 14 percent reported having placed at least one black child with a white family; 34 percent reported having placed at least one black-white child with a white family.

In personal interviews with social workers Cecelia Sudia was told that most biracial children have white mothers. The examples given in newspaper articles and scholarly research both commonly mention white mothers.

Ladner, *Mixed Families,* pp. 3, 40, 43, 132, 137, 164, 209, 230. Marsha Hohm and Judy Miner, "Interracial Adoptions in the Washington, D.C., Area" (Paper, 1970). Gary Brooten, "Multiracial Family," *New York Times Magazine* September 26, 1971, p. 80. Betty Medsger, "Black Groups Now Resisting Adoptions by White Families," *Washington Post* May 31, 1972. Personal communication from Cecelia Sudia. Simon and Altstein, *Transracial Adoption,* p. 26. Grow and Shapiro, *Black Children, White Parents,* p. 28. Ryo Suzuki and Marilyn Horn, "Follow-up Study of Negro-White Adoptions" (Paper from L.A. County Bureau of Adoptions, June 1967), p. 3.

29. Child Welfare League of America, *Standards for Adoption Service* (New York: CWLA, 1958), p. 24.

30. Esther B. Nordlie and Sheldon C. Reed, "Follow-up on Adoption Counseling for Children of Possible Racial Admixture," *Child Welfare* September 1962, p. 300.

31. CWLA, *Standards for Adoption Service,* p. 24; "Revised Sections,"

memo dated 1963; *Standards for Adoption Service,* p. 34. Copyright 1968 CWLA. Reprinted with permission.

32. Simon and Altstein, *Transracial Adoption,* p. 74. Grow and Shapiro, *Black Children, White Parents,* p. 42. E. Raskies, "An Exploration Study of the Characteristics of Adoptive Parents of Mixed Race Children in the Montreal Area" (Master's thesis, University of Montreal, 1963). Laurence L. Falk, "A Comparative Study of Transracial and Inracial Adoptions," *Child Welfare* February 1970, pp. 82-88.

33. Elizabeth Herzog, Cecelia Sudia, Jane Harwood, and Carol Newcomb, *Families for Black Children, An Experience Survey* (Washington: Government Printing Office, 1971), p. 42.

34. Edmond D. Jones, "On Transracial Adoption of Black Children," *Child Welfare* March 1972, p. 158.

35. Betty Medsger, "Black Groups Now Resisting Black Adoptions by White Families." Reprinted with permission from the *Washington Post.*

36. Roger Kahn, "Black and White," *Children* July-August 1971, p. 160.

37. Linda Katz, "Transracial Adoption: Some Guidelines," *Child Welfare* March 1974, pp. 180-187. Herzog et al., *Families for Black Children,* p. 43.

38. Ladner, *Mixed Families,* pp. 75, 86; Jones, "On Transracial Adoption of Black Children," p. 162; and Simon and Altstein, *Transracial Adoption,* p. 50f.

39. CWLA, *Standards for Adoption Service,* p. 92.

40. National Association of Black Social Workers (NABSW), "NABSW Opposes Trans-Racial Adoption" (Undated reprint of the NABSW). Reprinted with permission. Also personal correspondence from the New York chapter of the NABSW, September 7, 1977.

41. Simon and Altstein, *Transracial Adoption,* p. 19.

42. See note 7.

43. Annie Lee Sandusky, Jane Harwood Rea, Ursula Gallagher, and Elizabeth Herzog, *Families for Black Children: The Search for Adoptive Parents,* Part II, "Programs and Projects" (Washington: Government Printing Office, 1972), p. 12; and unpublished statistics for New York City agencies available from Graham Windham, One Park Avenue, New York, New York, for 1974 through 1976.

44. Michele Burgen, "Should Whites Adopt Black Children?" *Ebony* December 1977, p. 63.

45. Miriam Vieni, "White Parents—Black Children," *Adoptalk* 3, no. 1 (March 1978): 23.

46. Nutt and Snyder, "Trans-Racial Adoption," p. 33ff.

47. Simon and Altstein, *Transracial Adoption,* p. 46.

48. Ladner, *Mixed Families,* p. 202.

49. Grow and Shapiro, *Black Children, White Parents,* p. 73.

50. Simon and Altstein, *Transracial Adoption,* p. 71, 96f; Ladner, *Mixed Families,* p. 178.

51. Laurance L. Falk, "Comparative Study of Transracial and Inracial Adoptions," *Child Welfare* 29, no. 2 (February 1970): 84.

52. Ibid., p. 85; Ladner, *Mixed Families,* p. 202; Simon and Altstein, *Transracial Adoption,* p. 95f.

53. Ladner, ibid., pp. xiii, 10, 203f.

54. Ibid., p. 95f.

55. Brooten, "The Multiracial Family," p. 80 © 1971 by the New York Times Company. Reprinted by permission.

56. Hohm and Miner, "Interracial Adoptions in the Washington, D.C., Area," p. 18.

57. Ladner, *Mixed Families,* p. 211.

58. Simon and Altstein, *Transracial Adoption,* p. 95.

59. Falk, "Comparative Study of Transracial and Inracial Adoptions," p. 87.

60. Ladner, *Mixed Families,* pp. 206, 209f.

61. Jones, "On Transracial Adoption of Black Children," p. 159.

62. B. Drummond Ayers, "Rift over Pastor in Plains Linked to Adopted Boy," *New York Times* February 24, 1977.

63. Ladner, *Mixed Families,* pp. 193, 195.

64. Loretta Leone, "They Adopted Multi-racial Children," *Boston Sunday Herald Traveler* June 16, 1968, sec. 4, p. 6.

65. Lawrence L. Shornack, "Adoptive Parent Study" available from Open Door Society of Connecticut, Inc., P.O. Box 478, Hartford, Connecticut 06101. See pp. 14-16. Reprinted with permission.

66. Ladner, *Mixed Families*, pp. 4, 206.

67. Brooten, "The Multiracial Family," p. 80 © 1971 by the New York Times Company. Reprinted by permission.

68. Ladner, *Mixed Families,* p. 212.

69. George Gallup, "Tolerance of Mixed Marriages Increases," *Washington Post* November 19, 1972.

70. Alicia Howard, David D. Royse, and John A. Skerl, "Transracial Adoption: The Black Community Perspective," *Social Work* May 1977, p. 186.

71. Simon and Altstein, *Transracial Adoption,* p. 77; and Shornack, "Adoptive Parent Study," p. 4.

72. Grow and Shapiro, *Black Children, White Parents,* pp. vi, 47.

73. Ibid., p. 29.

74. Ibid., p. 52.

75. Ladner, *Mixed Families,* p. 23.

76. Jones, "On Transracial Adoption of Black Children," p. 160.

77. Ladner, *Mixed Families,* p. 5.

78. Ibid., p. 110.

79. Amuzie Chimezie, "Transracial Adoption of Black Children," *Social Work* July 1975, p. 300.

80. Grow and Shapiro, *Black Children, White Parents,* p. 60. Reprinted with permission.

81. Falk, "Comparative Study of Transracial and Inracial Adoptions," p. 85f.

82. Simon and Altstein, *Transracial Adoption,* p. 98f.

83. Grow and Shapiro, *Black Children, White Parents,* pp. 110, 144. Reprinted with permission.

84. Ibid., p. 34.

85. Ibid., pp. 149, 177. Reprinted with permission.

86. Ibid., p. 53.

87. Ibid., p. 56.

88. Simon and Altstein, *Transracial Adoption,* p. 31.

89. Jones, "On Transracial Adoption of Black Children."

90. Ladner, *Mixed Families,* p. 130.

91. Ibid., pp. 23, 31, 142.

92. Ibid., p. 143f.

93. Simon and Altstein, *Transracial Adoption,* p. 97f.

94. Marlene Daehlin as told to Levi Keidel, "We Adopted a Negro Child," *National Adoptalk* March-April 1970, p. 5. Reprinted with permission from the original publisher, the *Michigan Christian Advocate.*

95. Simon and Altstein, *Transracial Adoption,* p. 148 and chap. 6.

96. Teresa Chebuhar, "In Mixed-Race Adoptions, Home Stability Is Vital," *Seattle Times* August 15, 1976.

97. Grow and Shapiro, *Black Children, White Parents,* p. 102.

98. Scarr and Weinberg, "IQ Performance of Black Children Adopted by White Families," p. 736f.

99. Chebuhar, "In Mixed-Race Adoptions."

100. Scarr and Weinberg, "IQ Performance of Black Children Adopted by White Families," p. 736f.

101. Simon and Altstein, *Transracial Adoption,* p. 105. Shornack asked 54 white parents who had adopted black children whether, if they could do it over again, they would adopt a black child; 46 answered in the affirmative. Shornack, "Adoptive Parent Study," p. 27.

102. Ladner, *Mixed Families,* p. 122.

103. CWLA, *Newsletter,* Spring 1973. A variety of comments from social workers indicates that the cutback in placements with white families is in direct response to the criticisms of the black social workers. Opportunity, 1972-1974, and personal correspondence from Leroy D. Zimmerman of Lutheran Family and Children's Services of Missouri, May 31, 1972.

104. Statistics on black adoptions published annually by Opportunity. The data are incomplete, but they are the best available.

105. Joseph Morgenstern, "The New Face of Adoption," *Newsweek* September 13, 1971, p. 67.

106. Ibid.

107. Ladner, *Mixed Families,* p. 113.

108. Angela Terrell, "Interracial Adoption," *Washington Post* December 10, 1972.

109. Ladner, *Mixed Families,* p. 245.

How It Can Be Done

Why would anyone adopt a family of six children?

John and Cathy Williams, who did, often are asked this question.

"The children needed us and we needed them," answers Williams, his tone indicating surprise that some people make a big deal of it.

The Williamses' new family, a young boy and his five sisters, had been pictured in a *Detroit News* article. (The names used have been changed to retain privacy.)

"My wife had talked to me about adopting for years. When I saw these children, I just took the paper in and laid it on her bed. She said, 'Oh, John, those are our children!'"

Homes for Black Children, the adoption agency, was thinking of finding two families who were close friends and would adopt three children each.

"Don't split them," Mr. and Mrs. Williams pleaded. "We want to adopt them all."

Because the six children had suffered severe neglect, the social worker asked a psychiatrist to evaluate the adoption as well as any need for individual therapy.

Considering what they had endured, the doctor said, the children were in very good shape. But he didn't think one family should tackle the job of adopting all six.

But Mr. and Mrs. Williams still insisted. "We know we can handle it. We want them all." Half-convinced, the social worker persuaded the psychiatrist to accompany her to the Williamses' home.

When they left, the psychiatrist had reversed his position. "This is no usual family," he said. "I believe they can do it."

A number of things probably influenced this decision:

Mrs. Williams came from a family of 19 children.

Their big house stands on a five-acre lot, with a pool and plenty of room for children and animals.

The Williamses' idea of a perfect vacation had been to fill their motor home with grandchildren and take off.

Both Mr. and Mrs. Williams worked as custodians for a college. She resigned when the children moved in, and recently said, "I'm happier than when I was young."[1]

The adoption is working out very well. The Williamses are a remarkable couple, and the Detroit agency which placed the children with them is a remarkable agency. A more conventional agency might have turned down the Williamses. The adopted children are fairly young, ranging in age from 2 to 10; and, after all, the Williamses are middle-aged, and they already have grandchildren. The Williamses do not have many financial resources; he is a custodian, and now that the children are adopted, she is no longer working. (Her quitting work would have pleased a traditional adoption agency.)

Because of the severe neglect the children had suffered, a more cautious agency might have reasoned that no one couple could be expected to cope with the problems that might arise with trying to raise all six children together. Fortunately for the Williamses and their six newly adopted children, Homes for Black Children, the agency charged with placing the children, was no ordinary adoption agency.

Homes for Black Children probably had its beginnings in the smoldering ashes of 1967. Once the riot was over, those involved with social policy sought with special energy to find ways to alleviate the social inequality and bad conditions which the riots had protested. The United Foundation set up an Urban Crisis Fund to finance special projects.

For those who knew the social welfare field, an obvious area of need was adoption. In 1968, incomplete statistics indicated that there were more than 300 black children in the Detroit area who were available for adoption. This was more than three times the number of black children who had been placed for adoption the previous year by all 13 agencies reporting to the United Community Services of metropolitan Detroit.[2]

In addition to the more than 300 black children who were legally free for adoption at that time, several hundred other black children for whom adoption appeared to be the realistic alternative were living in foster homes. No effort had been made to free these foster children for adoption because it was thought that adoptive homes could not be found. A number of the black children had already waited five or ten years for permanent homes.

Homes were not even being found for infants.

> Every boarding home spot in the community available to black children was almost continuously filled. The private maternity homes, a program to provide medical care for indigent mothers, and a continuing education program for pregnant teenagers in the inner city all had the same problem.[3]

Even when the mother was pleading for help, an Illegitimacy Study Committee set up by the United Community Services was often unable to find an agency, public or private, that was willing to accept relinquishment and take the responsibility for finding an adoptive homes for a black infant. If she were really desperate, a young mother might be advised to abandon her baby in the hospital; then maybe the state would take custody of the child. "Dozens of black unwed mothers were denied service of any kind and were forced to take babies home even though they knew it was impossible to provide adequately for them."[4]

In response to this tremendous need and moved by a new consciousness created by the civil rights movement of the 1960s, the Urban Crisis Fund of the United Foundation of Detroit granted funds to set up a special program through Lutheran Children's Friend Society to find adoptive homes for black children.

Skeptics wondered about what the program could accomplish. After all, "black people don't adopt." Those who thought otherwise pointed out that orphanages are a European, not African, institution. Black families have always made room for children who needed homes; so, of course, given an opportunity, black people would adopt through an agency.

The grant from the Urban Crisis Fund provided funds for a program director and five social workers. Operations were started in 1969 with a goal of making 100 placements in the first year. This goal was met in nine months. After two years' existence, a total of 238 black children had been given permanent homes, and the program called Homes for Black Children was on its way to becoming an independent agency.

Says agency director Sydney Duncan, "There is no reason why this couldn't be done elsewhere or couldn't have been done before. There are plenty of qualified black families who'd like to adopt a child. There always have been."[5]

Spreading the Word

Homes for Black Children did all the things other adoption agencies do. It just did some of them in a different way. The first step in getting applicants was to notify the black community that the agency was there and looking for black families to adopt. Some adoption publicity aimed at black families has been insulting, particularly that which implies that black families are not interested in children and white families are. Homes for Black Children built its news stories around the fact that black families have always adopted children in large numbers, although the arrangements often have been informal.

The initial publicity centered on the black program director and the program name, Homes for Black Children. These two factors led to black community identification and assured blacks that here was an agency designed to serve the black community.

Publicity included the agency's purpose and notice that the agency did not charge a fee for adoption. Also included was the fact that the agency did not require families to be home owners or have a specific income or religion. Thus prospective adopters were not frightened off by incorrect impressions of the agency's requirements.

As a public service, Michigan Consolidated Gas Company financed a film on Homes for Black Children and distributed it nationally. The film has been used both to recruit black families and to inform other agencies about Homes for Black Children's approach to adoption.

The *Detroit News* column "A Child Is Waiting," which found the Williams family, has been and is a key means through which Homes for Black Children finds adoptive families. Successful adopters have become important informal recruiters for the agency also.

Because of all the good publicity, both through the mass media and by word of mouth, the social workers at Homes for Black Children never did have to get very involved with recruiting.

Appropriate Processing

Homes for Black Children has had very good publicity, both in Detroit and on the national scene. But good publicity is never enough. In order to be success-ful, Homes for Black Children social workers had to develop techniques to deal with the distrust and anxiety with which black clients, wary of a rebuff even from a black-oriented agency, would approach them. The black identification of the agency was an important help but not sufficient in itself. The social workers had to develop a system for processing the adoptive applicants and think through their requirements for adoptive parenthood. Homes for Black Children staff have defined parenting as "providing love, guidance, protection, and meeting the basic emotional and physical needs of a child."[6]

In the adoption interviews, the worker tries to get to know how a particular family lives and what their expectations for adoption are. Interviews are not conducted on a therapeutic level.

Applicants must have medical examinations and submit employment verifi-cations and five references. Adoptive couples have to be legally married, 18 years of age or older (the age of majority in Michigan), capable of supporting a child, and able to give love and parental guidance. The agency has set no hard-and-fast rules on subjects such as home ownership, fertility, family size, or previous marriages. Single persons are permitted to adopt.

The agency does not attempt to match parents and children on skin color unless the family happens to request it.[7]

The agency is looking for something other than a two-car garage and a dish-washer. The question of whether a couple is financially able to care for a child is based on how that family uses its resources, and placements have been made with families whose incomes go as low as $5000, in families where the parents have grade school educations, and in families where the father works in a low-skill occupation.

Homes for Black Children has also tapped the black middle class in Detroit and made placements with families with incomes of $40,000 and above.

Workers at Homes for Black Children are aware of the realities of the black family's experiences in the United States. They know, for example, that many black men change jobs often in order to get into a higher income bracket and therefore do not take such movement as an indication of instability.

In helping applicants get the necessary papers, Homes for Black Children social workers have gone all out. Many families, especially those coming from the South, do not have such things as birth certificates, a copy of their marriage license, or a death certificate on a deceased spouse. Workers have spent many hours helping families learn how to obtain these papers. If a missing paper cannot be located, the worker tries to get affidavits or other types of verification. This extra investment has enabled many families to adopt through Homes for Black Children who either had been turned down by another agency or were afraid to pursue their interest in adoption because they felt that they did not qualify.

Director Duncan feels that it is very important to respond to applicants in the same way in which they apply. For example, when a family calls up in response to a newspaper article about a particular child, the family is showing concern about that child as a human being. Homes for Black Children responds on that same human level, setting up an appointment within a week, either at the caller's home or at the agency, whichever the caller prefers. During the first interview, the applicant learns about Homes for Black Children and adoption, and the agency begins learning about the applicant.

If the applicants seem as if they might be intimidated by the application blank, the worker helps them fill it out. Otherwise the worker leaves it with the family. The personal contact before the application blank is given out means that the application blank is seen as part of a joint sharing process rather than as a bureaucratic device for getting rid of people. Homes for Black Children never puts paperwork between the social worker and the applicant family.[8] Before the home study is through, Homes for Black Children knows a lot about the family, but the application form is kept simple and unintimidating.[9]

Homes for Black Children's advice to other agencies is to avoid sending out application blanks in response to an inquiry. A good prospective family seeing questions such as "Have you had a physician examine you to determine whether you are sterile?" and "Do you own your home?" assumes that only one answer is correct and gives up before having begun.

At Homes for Black Children, the applicants often choose to have their first visit in their own homes; they feel more comfortable there. Later interviews between the worker and family are scheduled in the office at times convenient for the family. This has meant that Homes for Black Children does not function on a nine-to-five basis, but stays open twice a week in the evenings for the convenience of those families who work and need evening appointments. The agency is located in a black neighborhood, easily accessible to public transportation.

The agency has experimented with both group and individual interviews in the adoption process. When applicants miss an appointment, follow-up phone calls are made to let families know that the agency is interested in their desire to adopt a child. The assumption is never made that a missed appointment means a lack of interest in adoption.

Homes for Black Children helps keep adoption costs for their adopting families down by not charging a fee. Michigan law permits adoption without the involvement of a lawyer, so Homes for Black Children, like other Michigan agencies, helps clients take the necessary legal steps; as a result, no client has to pay a lawyer's fee.

Homes for Black Children has always taken great care to hire qualified staff. When the agency was founded, all the staff members hired had experience in working in the inner city and with black families. They felt comfortable relating to the experiences of black family life.

Right from the beginning, Homes for Black Children hired both white and black social workers. The agency has found that competent, interested white staff who are familiar with the black community have no problems communicating with black families. The agency, of course, has always had black staff in visible administrative positions to whom black clients could relate if they felt a white worker did not understand their life situation.

In their first year of operation, Homes for Black Children placed one black child with a white family.[10] After that, the staff focused on the black community, referring white families who wanted to adopt black children to other agencies doing interracial adoptions.

Homes for Black Children has received many small contributions from community people to support their adoption program. This has been formalized now into an organization called Friends of Homes for Black Children. The funds raised by this group have been useful in giving emergency help to families and children in crises.

Winning Cooperation from Other Agencies

Homes for Black Children (HBC) was created as a backstop for other agencies. HBC provides no maternity and counseling services; rather it accepts children on referral from other agencies which need help in finding adoptive homes.

In the beginning, HBC had to establish its credentials as a competent child-placing organization. Otherwise, dependent as it was on the referrals of other agencies, it would not have survived.

Homes for Black Children established its competence in a variety of ways.
(1) All the social workers had master's degrees, a standard of training not met
by most other Detroit agencies at that time. (2) The social workers were
experienced in working with black families and were sensitive to their needs.
(3) The adoptive home studies were very carefully done. (4) Homes for Black
Children had the sponsorship and active support of a respected Detroit agency,
Lutheran Children's Friend Society, and its Director of Social Service, Clarence
Fischer. (5) After a few months of operation, HBC's record spoke for itself:
100 children placed in nine months.

The potential adoptive families had always been there. The problem was
that some of the other Detroit agencies, hampered by the false belief that blacks
do not adopt, had not actively sought black adoptive homes. Other agencies
had tried to find black adopters but had unfortunately eliminated many potential adopters by inappropriate adoption criteria.

Homes for Black Children easily could have been sidetracked into trying
to change the other adoption agencies in the area. Instead HBC focused on
finding adoptive families for children. In the process of doing this, of course,
Homes for Black Children gently led other agencies to see how it could be done.
This approach worked. In the first year of operation, Homes for Black Children
arranged placements in cooperation with 13 different agencies.[11]

Homes for Black Children's crucial support in the first year came from
Catholic Social Services of Wayne County, which provided 80 of the first 125
children HBC placed. Without the Catholic Social Services' cooperation, HBC's
initial placement record would not have been nearly as spectacular; and with a
less spectacular record, Homes for Black Children's impact on the other Detroit
agencies would have been considerably reduced.

In about two years, almost all the Detroit Adoption agencies had increased
their placements of black children, through either referral to Homes for Black
Children or their own recruitment efforts or both.

Now Homes for Black Children gets referrals from all over Michigan. The
Michigan state social service manual says to all the state adoption units that if a
black home cannot be found, call Homes for Black Children. Private agencies
outside Detroit also refer children to HBC. Some agencies with religious sponsorship still will not make placements outside their own sponsoring religion but
will nonetheless permit Homes for Black Children to do so with a referred child.

Changing the Courts

Homes for Black Children used the same pragmatic approach with the courts
that it used with other agencies. Unreasonable rules were challenged by qualified
applicants. For example, one of the unwritten requirements of a court had been
that applicants should be married at least five years and be between the ages of

30 and 40. Homes for Black Children brought in a couple where the wife had had a hysterectomy; she was not quite 21, and he was 25. By the unwritten requirements, the couple was ten years too soon. But it was obvious they would be good parents, and they were permitted to adopt. Other later applicants then also benefited.

There had been an unwritten rule that adoptive applicants had to be citizens. Homes for Black Children brought in a Canadian couple, and they were approved. HBC brought in a medical student from Ghana and his wife; the couple planned to return to Ghana in five years. They were refused. Then HBC brought in a Cuban family who were not citizens. However, a United States law provided that the Cubans could never be deported. This couple was permitted to adopt. Homes for Black Children always persisted; and once a rule changed, the change worked for other adoptive applicants as well.

Sometimes other social agencies thought that the courts had views and policies which the judges themselves did not hold. Homes for Black Children learned that their staff could go directly to the judge to find out firsthand what policies were. This approach was invaluable in dispelling myths, in this case propagated by social agencies.[12]

Changes over a Decade

In the first few years of the adoption program, HBC placed over 100 children each year. Then the number of children placed per year began to fall. Learning from HBC's example, other agencies had begun placing more black children. With the change in the abortion situation, fewer unwanted babies were being born. Referrals of children from inside Michigan fell. Agencies outside the state were beginning to hear about Homes for Black Children, and HBC began placing more and more children from out of state. In time HBC faced the fact that they were only funded to place children from agencies inside Michigan and drew back from most placements involving out-of-state children.

During the period at the end of the Vietnam war, HBC did receive special funds which were used to place six black Vietnamese children and some other children from other states. However, in recent years, HBC's basic focus has been on Michigan. The agency's director finds this restriction acceptable. With older and handicapped children, she feels that placement is more like a marriage and that the family and child need time to get acquainted without the pressure which expensive travel costs can add.

By 1978 HBC had a waiting list of about a year for families for a healthy child under school age. HBC is not able to place every child referred to them, but they have taken on some difficult cases and succeeded impressively. The Williams family and their six children are a good example. In 1976, over half of the children whom HBC placed were handicapped.

HBC has also helped families legalize informal adoptions. Informal adoptions occur when a birth parent gives a child directly to another person.

A 73-year-old widower terminally ill with cancer has approached HBC, asking them to find an adoptive home for his 8-year-old daughter. He wants the adoption completed soon so that he can die knowing his daughter will be cared for. It will be a difficult situation in which the adoptive family will have to make special efforts to keep their adopted daughter in touch with her biological father until his death. Homes for Black Children is willing to accept the challenge to try to find such a home.

As the supply of healthy preschoolers available for adoption has been reduced, HBC's adoption program has diminished and changed direction. Now there is more focus on older and handicapped children. These placements are more difficult, but the staff members at HBC are willing to take risks. They know the alternative is that the child will grow up in foster homes, never having a permanent relationship with a parent.

In 1974 HBC started a new program called the Black Family Preservation Program, which was designed to help families of abused and neglected children. By providing supportive counseling and strengthening families, HBC helps make it possible for many of the families to stay together.

Director Duncan is concerned about developing a balanced program. Too much effort put into adoption draws children into a system where they do not belong. Too much emphasis on family preservation can result in an inappropriate struggle to keep all children with their parents. Her goal is to help the Detroit community create a variety of programs so that more than one alternative is available for the family and child in crisis.

Notes

1. Ruth Carlton, "36 Find Homes in 1977 through 'A Child Is Waiting,'" *Detroit News* December 25, 1977, p. 1E. Reprinted with permission.

2. The material for this chapter is taken from printed material distributed by Homes for Black Children; a personal interview with the Director, Sydney Duncan; Clarence D. Fischer, "Homes for Black Children, *Child Welfare* February 1971, pp. 108-111; Iris S. Jones, "Agency in Detroit Eliminates Adoption Obstacles," *Ebony* June 1976, p. 53ff; and Flora Cunha, "What about Black Parent Adoptions?" *National Adoptalk* May-June 1971, pp. 1, 6.

3. Fischer, ibid., p. 108f. Reprinted with permission.

4. Ibid., p. 109.

5. Joseph Morgenstern, "The New Face of Adoption," *Newsweek* September 13, 1971, p. 68. Copyright 1971 by Newsweek, Inc. All rights reserved. Reprinted by permission.

6. "Homes for Black Children," mimeographed and distributed by the agency, May 1974, p. 4.

7. Cunha, "What about Black Parent Adoptions?" p. 6.
8. Jones, "Agency in Detroit Eliminates Adoption Obstacles," p. 59.
9. Cunha, "What about Black Parent Adoptions?" p. 6.
10. Fischer, "Homes for Black Children," p. 110.
11. Ibid., p. 111.
12. Cunha, "What about Black Parent Adoptions?" p. 6.

Epilog

This book has been about the thousands of children who are homeless and who need adoptive homes now. Their need for a family should be met. But we also need to look at our system of social services and examine the ways in which that system itself breaks up families and creates homeless children.

Let me illustrate with a hypothetical example which includes almost every bad practice a foster care program can have. A low-income family has a crisis and cannot care for their children with their limited resources. The children are placed in one or more foster homes. The possibility of placement with interested relatives is not explored prior to placement with strangers. The children are separated and placed in homes quite distant from their parents' home. Few or no funds are available to help the parents pay the travel costs of visiting their children or for trial home visits. The parents are not encouraged to visit their children or informed of the importance of maintaining contact to prevent the termination of parental rights. When a problem occurs at one of the foster homes, the parents are not informed as their child is moved from one foster home to the next. The parents are not informed of their children's progress or important events such as a graduation. When the parents are unhappy about the way their children are being treated in a foster home, they have no ombudsperson to whom to bring their complaint. The parents are not even informed of the procedures by which to request the return of their children. The children do not have the same caseworker, so no worker is responsible for thinking about the children as a group. The children are visited once a year or less by their different caseworkers. The caseworkers make no attempt to contact the parents to help them get their children back.

Perhaps no foster care system really embodies all these bad practices (although some must come fairly close). The purpose here is just to illustrate the kinds of problems that can occur and point out the divisive impact foster care can have on a family.

The example assumes that the children and parents had to be separated. In fact, it has been found that foster care can be avoided when families are offered necessary supportive services—emergency housing, homemakers, crisis counseling.

Our welfare system encourages poor couples not to live together and marry because under most circumstances only a mother and children can be eligible for assistance. The low-income, single mother runs a high risk of having to put her children in foster care when she is hit by a crisis such as a severe illness.

In our rhetoric we value the family, but in our practice we do not. For example, programs which separate families (foster care) are available in every county; programs which provide concrete services to keep families together, such as emergency housing and homemakers, are few and far between. Our financial aid programs encourage couples not to marry, creating a family structure (single mothers) less able to handle a crisis without help. Our foster care programs take care of the physical needs of children (usually) but do little to bring parents and children back together again.

We need to find adoptive homes for children who need them. We also need to reform our social welfare system so that additional homeless children are not needlessly generated.

Appendix A
Birth Mothers Speak Out

Some adopted adults are now seeking information about their birth mothers. For the most part, the birth mothers have been silent, but here and there they are speaking out. The first article reproduced here is about a mother who gave up her three children for adoption and then seventeen years later, after counseling, wanted to tell her story. The second article is an anonymous letter from a mother who does not want to be found.

Why One Mother Gave Up Her Children[a]

For years, Marva Villegas would simply answer no when anyone asked if she had children because that was easier then enduring the expressions of surprise, horror or pity that came when she offered the truth.

Seventeen years ago she put her three children—ages 5, 4 and 2—up for adoption. She has not seen them since.

Today, at age 41, she is a spirited, confident woman who works as a salesperson. She is telling her story, she says, because she wants people to understand why a woman would relinquish her children, and what she goes through.

She is also trying to help publicize the Los Angeles County Department of Adoption's new service for women who have put their children up for adoption.

Mrs. Villegas recently sent a note to the Department of Adoptions, updating her records and indicating that they could open her file to anyone making inquiry. If her children were trying to find her, she wanted to make their job easy. (Present California law prevents agencies from opening adoption records, even if both the birth mother and adult adoptees desire to do so.)

Because of her note, Department of Adoptions social worker Joan Podrow called Mrs. Villegas last December.

Mrs. Podrow was able to provide specific information about where Mrs. Villegas' children had been placed. The adoptive father 17 years ago was a 30-year-old lawyer; the mother was a college graduate and pianist described as being "feminine" and "a homemaker."

Mrs. Podrow also invited Mrs. Villegas to join a new county-sponsored counseling group being formed for birth mothers who had given up their children for adoption.

---

[a]Barry Siegel, "Why One Mother Gave Up Her Children," *Los Angeles Times* February 27, 1978, part IV. ©1978, Reprinted by permission.

Feeling Guilty

"We found it was a good idea for these mothers to talk with each other about their experiences," explains Mrs. Podrow. "They mostly just express feelings of guilt. Even though they knew it was the only way to go, they sense they did something wrong. They forget the very real reasons why they gave up their children in the first place."

Mrs. Villegas agrees this is why she is telling her story. "Society forgets that the birth mother is hurting," she says. "People look at her and say, 'How could she do it? It's so horrible, so unnatural.' For years and years, this bothered me. I would tell people I didn't have kids. But now if I'm judged, if people don't understand, that's their problem."

As she talks in the offices of the county Department of Adoptions, her self-assurance and self-knowledge distance her from the past. She recalls her earlier years almost as if they involved another person—a person she knew slightly.

Marva Villegas grew up in Compton and married a sailor in 1954, when she was 17. "I was in the 11th grade and the high school asked me to leave, because a married woman was considered a bad influence on the other students. I didn't argue."

Her first child, Allan, was born the next year; the second, Bobby, came one year later.

"I always had figured that the next thing after getting married was to have children," she explains. "I always just wanted kids."

But her marriage to the sailor soon foundered. They separated for the first time when Mrs. Villegas was pregnant with Bobby; there followed several attempted reconciliations. During one of them, she became pregnant for a third time. In 1958, at the age of 21, she had her third child, Raymond.

Soon after, she left her husband permanently. "That's when things really started getting rough. I was living on a $157 Navy allotment check and just was not settled. My mother and stepdad lived in Mexico; my own dad said I should put the kids up for adoption. I was taking in ironing and baby-sitting to live."

A Remembered Face

Then her husband left the Navy on a medical discharge, so her military allotment checks stopped.

"I was 22, broke, with an 11th grade education, no job and three kids. I went to the Welfare Department. I don't know the man's name I spoke with there, but I still remember his face today. I hated him. He told me I couldn't get aid until I had been without support for 90 days. He was so nasty. I never went back."

She finally found a job in a beer bar, working 6 p.m. to 2 a.m. Every night she would leave her children with a girlfriend.

"Sometimes the kids were fed, sometimes they weren't. I'd find them in bed with their clothes on or all wet. When they got up, I'd be sleeping, so I never saw them. We moved every other month because I couldn't pay the rent. It was such a disaster, I couldn't believe it."

Mrs. Villegas says her father continued to argue that the children should be put up for adoption. "I wasn't ready to face that idea, but things just got worse."

"The children were 4, 3 and 1½ then. The 4-year-old started wetting the bed again, and I knew it was from lack of security. I had no money to feed them anything but macaroni, beans or pancakes. In the back of my mind I started thinking about a temporary foster home."

In June 1960, she finally went to the county Department of Adoptions where she began a series of long talks with a social worker. "She was a super person. She gave me money that first day to buy groceries. That endeared her to me. I still just wanted a temporary foster home, but as we talked, I started to decide that adoption was better than switching the kids from home to home."

"No Chance with Me"

One day she returned to her apartment and told the children that she was going to get them new parents.

"The two youngest didn't know what I was talking about. The oldest, who was 4, was very willing to get a new father but not a new mother. He said he wanted me to come, too."

"I would talk to Allan until he cried, or I cried, or we both cried," *she says.* "I couldn't give them anything. They needed something more stable. But they couldn't understand that. I felt terrible, but I had to do it. They had no chance with me."

On July 5, 1960, she woke the children up and helped them pack their belongings. "I remember little about it. I just remember that I wanted to make sure they had their books and things they were familiar with. It seems odd now, but I kept thinking about their books."

At the Department of Adoptions, she was left alone with her children in a large room.

"I was okay until I was alone with them. Then I started crying. Allan just put his hand on my shoulder and said, 'Don't cry, mommy.'"

"The hardest part was when I went home alone. I felt that the inside of

*my body was so empty. I can never describe it. I've never felt anything like that
again."*

   *"The night I gave up my children, I went out and got drunk by myself. I
was alone, totally alone. I called my dad and told him what I had done and that
I wanted to come over and talk. He said no, that he didn't want to talk about
it."*

   "For months," Mrs. Villegas says, *"I just cried and cried. The children were
first put in a temporary foster home, so I could have seen them, or even taken
them back. Oh, did I want them back! But I've always been able to see the facts.
I had nothing for them, was 23, confused and scared."*

   She never saw her children again. She signed the official adoption papers
August 25.

   Soon after, she left California, traveling with a boyfriend and girlfriend from
city to city, hitchhiking and taking jobs by the week. She thought about suicide.
She could not stand to watch little children at play. She remarried, but that did
not work out.

   *"I was trying to fill a need. I finally came to understand that this need—for
my kids—would never be filled. It is still with me. But it no longer influences
my day-to-day life."*

Fourth Marriage

She returned to California after almost three years on the road and took a job
with a company where she has remained for 15 years. She recently switched
from her position as product manager to sales and is married to her fourth
husband.

   Although she settled down, Mrs. Villegas never had any more children.
When she was 29, she had to have a hysterectomy.

   *"I had always said I wasn't going to have more kids, but in the back of my
mind I always thought I would. Then I had to have the operation. I felt
guilty and wondered whether this was my punishment."*

   Mrs. Villegas says she thought about adopting children, *"but the husbands
I chose were not father material."* Her current husband already has children,
she explains, and wants no more.

   Last September, Mrs. Villegas joined ALMA (Adoptees Liberty Movement
Association) so her children could locate her if they wanted. She is trying to
decide whether she should actively look for them.

   *"Right from the start I had always carried the illusion that someday
they'd find me and I would be someone they'd want to know. I have no illusions
of being their mother, though."*

Unfinished Puzzle

Today, Allan would be 22, Bobby 21, Raymond 19. "I would like to explain to them why I gave them up, that it was not because I didn't want them. I also just want to know what they're doing, whether they have mustaches, whether I am a grandmother."

"I see a lot of young men. I stare into the eyes of anyone with blonde hair and wonder, is it one of them? When I go to a gas station I want to ask the guys their names. I once saw three boys together at Disneyland, but they had the wrong color eyes."

"Do you know the guy who plays Hutch on Starsky and Hutch?" she asks. "I think—I know—that's how my oldest son looks. I once went so far as finding out Hutch's age, but he was too old. Once I saw a picture in a newspaper that looked like Allan. I cut it out and tried to track it down through the Associated Press, but couldn't."

Mrs. Villegas shakes her head. "It's like an unfinished puzzle. I'd like to know how it turned out."

Would she do it again?

Mrs. Villegas does not hesitate. "I would do it again, even knowing what I would have to go through. I would just do it sooner, so that the kids could avoid all that hunger and insecurity. I could say what if—like what if I had had a job, or what if it had been 1978—but the fact is, I didn't and it wasn't."

After the article was published, Marva Villegas received a phone call from her two youngest sons. She met them and their adoptive mother, a woman who had been very supportive of their decision to call Mrs. Villegas.[b]

My Son, the Stranger[c]

I read the article, "Finding My Mother: An Adoptee's Journal," with a great deal of interest and a certain amount of concern. While I am completely sympathetic to the adoptees' needs to find their real mothers, to discover their roots and to answer the many emotional and intellectual questions that they have had to live with for most of their lives, I feel that another side of the story should be told.

---

[b]Helen Ramirez, Letter to the Editor, *Los Angeles Times* March 19, 1978, part VII, p. 17.

I gave birth to a son in 1970. He was adopted directly from the hospital, and, except for immediately after delivery, I never saw him. I was not and am not ashamed of these facts. While my decision to have my son adopted was not an easy one, it was made with the realization that I was not psychologically, socially or financially able to provide a child with the care necessary to help him grow into a happy and productive individual. I believe that my child is growing up with a mature, loving couple who love him more than I could have. (He was, after all, unwanted by me.) And that, quite simply, is that.

A Fading Memory

I do not often think of my son. I am happily married to a man who knows everything about my past but who cares much more for the present and the future. I have a career which keeps me busy and fulfilled. To both of us, the child I bore is a fading memory, a mysterious eternal baby who disappeared as mysteriously as it appeared. We do, of course, hope that the child is growing up strong and healthy, bright, loving and loved. But 20 years from now I do not intend to search for my child to find out what he looks like or if he has grown up to be strong and healthy, bright, loving and loved. I am not so wedded to the past that I have that need. Besides, if he isn't beautiful or bright or strong, what could I possibly do about it anyway? My recollection of my baby is as a tiny, red, screaming thing—frightening, incredible, beautifully impossible.

I am not callous, cold, or, in a constant framework of guilt, trying to forget a very important and undeniable fact of my life. If, 20 years from now, a grown man appeared at my door or called me on the phone, what could I do? What could I possibly offer to this person? Friendship, perhaps. But I am not so sure I would enjoy filling in all the mysterious details of his birth, or my family history, or providing an instant replay of my life for a total stranger. And he would be a stranger. I am, and forever will be, biological mother only. To me, a "mother" is more than the body and blood and genes from which one springs. My son's eyes may be the same color as mine, he may have my ability to sing—but his opportunities, his education, his experiences did not have a thing to do with me.

A Hidden Pregnancy

If, in the back of my mind, I had wished that my child should someday "find" me, I would not have gone to the trouble and expense of spending most of my pregnancy hidden away in an unwed mothers' home, using only an initial for a surname. When I gave birth to my child, I was known as "Mrs. Cooper" (not my real name) on hospital records. The adoption agency I worked with stressed complete anonymity. I did not resort to these measures out of shame or guilt, or to protect my family or myself from social repercussions. I felt, as I still feel, five years later, that my decision to have my child adopted included the necessity of relinquishing all claims—legal, social, financial and emotional. In return, I do not wish any claims to be made upon me.

I suppose my rambling defense has but one message: Adopted children, please don't think that your biological mother has The Answer. She may not, after all these years, remember the question.

Appendix B
One Agency's Publicity Program

Established in 1949, the Los Angeles County Department of Adoptions is a public agency serving a county with a population of more than 7 million.[a] The agency offers complete counseling, adoption, and postadoption services to birth parents, children, and adoptive parents.

The department is committed to the aggressive use of a variety of publicity techniques to attract adoptive applicants. In the 1960s, 87 percent of the department's placements were healthy Anglo infants. In 1978, about 87 percent of the department's adoptions involved children over 5; minority youngsters; children with serious medical, physical, and emotional problems; and sibling groups in which at least one child was over 6 years of age. The department's active public relations activities have helped change the character of the adoptive applicants to be more in line with the kind of children available for adoption.

With 115 social workers working out of six offices located in various parts of the county, the Department of Adoptions of Los Angeles County is one of the largest adoption agencies in the country. Its public relations activities could not be copied completely by other, smaller agencies, but parts of its program certainly could.

Major Themes in Recruitment Publicity

The department's publicity is concentrated on children with special needs—all those considered "hard to place." The publicity covers the traits and needs of such children. In publicizing individual children, the department attempts to highlight their positive attributes, indicating that they represent a larger group of children who need homes. The department also stresses that the problem of the child who is not adopted is a community problem which requires community action and involvement.

The department continually recruits families for minority infants, particularly black and Mexican-American, to ensure having sufficient homes, although they have been successful in placing almost all minority children under age 5 as soon as they are legally free.

The department emphasizes the types and traits of the adoptive parents

---

[a] Laine Waggoner, "Our Public Relations Program—Some Details of How It Works" (Department of Adoptions, County of Los Angeles, March 1978). Reprinted by permission.

sought and explains today's more flexible adoption requirements, the simpler procedure, and the financial aid available to some families. One of the best ways they do this is through human-interest stories which feature successful adoptive parents.

In California, adoption is within the reach of more middle- and low-income families because of the state's subsidy adoption program which has aided the adoption of over 2000 children since 1969. Consequently, the department minimizes the necessity of having a large income or owning a home.

Showing Parties

Several different types of special events are used to create excellent opportunities to disseminate information regarding the kinds of children available and the sort of parents they need. "Showing parties" are attended by children for whom homes are being sought and adults considering adoption of an older child. There is always a party atmosphere so that the children and adults can meet in a casual and informal fashion.

Occasionally, representatives of local churches, schools, and other community groups are invited so they may become better equipped to explain the department's program and needs to their own organizations.

The larger showing parties are usually cosponsored by the various regional auxiliaries of adoptive parents. "A Day at the Farm" has been held several times at a semirural location, where the children could see and play with many barnyard animals. "Ronald McDonald Day" has been hosted by a black adoptive parent who owns several McDonald's franchises. Ronald McDonald, the clown, has entertained; and there have been games, refreshments, and prizes for the children. At a recent "Fun Fair," prospective adoptive applicants took part in relay races and other such games as a means of meeting the children.

Adoption Day in Court

Since 1962 "Adoption Day in Court" has been an annual tradition and a hugely successful publicity event. It is held about two weeks before Christmas in Los Angeles Superior Court. For the occasion, media representatives are invited to interview and photograph or film the families waiting to enter the judge's chambers for their final decrees. Because of the built-in human interest and the closeness of Christmas, there is always an excellent media turnout.

The families and their attorneys are well prepared by the social workers beforehand. The families sign waivers in advance to indicate their willingness for publicity.

The department sends a photograph of each family to appropriate community, ethnic, religious, and employee publications. As a result of the countywide exposure, inquiries received by Applicant Intake increase dramatically for several months thereafter.

One of the advantages of adoption day as a recruitment device is that an ethnically, socially, and occupationally diverse group of parents are presented.

Black Adoptions Conference

Black adoptions conferences have succeeded in increasing inquiries from black families considerably. "Black Adoptions—A Community Affair" attracted particular media and community attention to a black applicant recruitment program. Held at a college located in a black community, the program included prominent speakers and information about adoption requirements and available children.

The Ben Hunter TV Show

The effectiveness of using communications media to recruit permanent homes for special-needs children has been proved time and again. It works because there are families that cannot accept the *concept* of adopting a hard-to-place child, but will respond on a very human level to "Maria" or "Johnny" when the *child as a person* is projected ahead of his or her psychological or medical problem. TV is the most effective and pervasive of the communications media because it reaches so many people on a very personal level. The department's most successful TV show has been the Ben Hunter's adoptions show, begun in 1967. By 1978, nearly 1100 hard-to-place children, ranging in age from infants to teenagers, had appeared on his show; and at least 840 of the children have been placed as a result.

The department maintains a degree of confidentiality by not using the children's last names when they appear on the Ben Hunter show. The children are, of course, very aware of their own surnames and somes slip and refer to them. So far, this has not caused any embarrassment or complication since nearly all the children shown are already legally free. The department does *not* televise a child who could be embarrassed by such exposure nor one who might be recognized by relatives or parents who live in the area.

The older children are quite well prepared for the TV appearance. The children usually have been involved in group meetings or individual sessions with their social workers, learning who they are, why they are in foster homes, the difference between foster care and adoption, what plans are being made for their futures, and so on.

Most of the children have seen the program before they themselves go on.

Generally, they are quite excited about it and will call it to the attention of neighbors and classmates. Furthermore, the day of the appearance becomes a fun outing day, with the opportunity to skip school and have lunch with their worker and refreshments after the show.

The youngsters appear on the show with the understanding that they are *representative* of the *kind of children* for whom the department is seeking homes. So they are not "on the spot," having to worry about whether there are any calls for them specifically. An information sheet is prepared for Hunter's use, so that he has something on which to base his chatty conversation with each child: about their likes and dislikes, their recent outings, friends, pets, and hobbies. Staff throughout the agency are notified of the children scheduled to appear and are encouraged to watch the show.

At the beginning, some staff members tended to be overly protective of their children. They expected the exposure to cause possible embarrassment or damage, but this never developed. When the staff began to see results in terms of placements and the ease and enjoyment of the children participating, they became more enthusiastic.

Hunter also regularly interviews staff members, foster parents, and adoptive parents to provide a wider perspective on the adoption scene.

Other TV Coverage

To take advantage of the limited free time available, the department prepares 10-, 20-, and 30-second spot announcements aimed at various audiences. They are sent to the stations to be read by their own announcers for about sixty days each. The department also supplies a color slide to be displayed on the screen, stating the agency name and central phone number. Public response to even the 10-second TV spot has been encouraging, with many callers saying, "I've been thinking about adoption for some time. Seeing your number stimulated me to pick up the phone."

The department has also filmed 30- and 60-second TV "commercials" using real adoptive parents and their children talking about the challenges and satis-factions of adoption. Recent efforts have been aimed at the black community, with callers responding positively to the warm and appealing parents depicted. The department has also created TV "spots" to recruit single parents and homes for older boys.

The department has arranged interviews for foster and adoptive parents, agency social workers and administrators, and sometimes legally free foster children, for discussion and public affairs shows on various stations.

TV news coverage is often sought for new programs or special events, such as the showing parties, providing all the children are free to be filmed. The department attempts to cooperate with media representatives whenever they need help in putting together a show.

Radio

Public service announcements on radio produce less dramatic results than TV. They serve best as a reminder. Celebrity spots can be effective, if it is a very recognizable voice.

Special promotions are sometimes prepared for ethnic-oriented or foreign language stations.

Newspapers and Magazines

Sprawling Los Angeles County is rather unique because of the number and variety of newspapers. It is served by 2 metropolitan dailies, 14 regional dailies, nearly 30 weekly and semiweekly chain operations, plus many small community, employee, special-interest, and ethnic newspapers, totaling more than 100 publications. The department relies heavily on these for publication of human-interest stories and the announcement of special events. Two local papers regularly run columns featuring a photograph and brief profile of a hard-to-place child.

Photographs of available children and of adoptive families have universal appeal and are vital elements in any effective bid for public attention. The department is careful that photographs are not used in areas where they would cause embarrassment for the child or family.

The department often provides magazine writers and editors with facts, figures, and interviews. Their theory is, "Get someone else to do the writing," because writing feature articles is a time-consuming task for which they lack staff.

Printed Materials

Recruitment appeals aimed at prospective foster parents, adoptive parents, and birth parents are contained in brochures, fact sheets, letters, and posters which are displayed in public places, distributed at group meetings, in high school and college classes, or mailed directly.

A brochure in the hand is often worth more than a feature story on TV or in a newspaper. This is because readers can take their time with the brochure's photographs and copy. The brochures attempt to answer commonly asked questions about adoptions and provide a handy listing of addresses and phone numbers of all the department's offices.

The copy is written in as simple and direct a fashion as possible, and the brochure covers are designed to be eye-catching.

Photographs command attention, especially those of children. Photographs usually are kept at local offices in loose-leaf binders for use by potential applicants.

A Slide Show Called "Headliners"

Since its inception in August 1976, the department has created about five "Headliners" slide shows a year. The response has been very favorable. "Headliners" are shown to potential applicants, to those in various stages of the study, and to workers with adoptive applicants so that they become more familiar with the children available. The children shown usually are among the most hard-to-place youngsters. Even an out-of-date "Headliners" is effective in showing the audience the types of children who usually wait the longest for homes. Six to eight children are featured in each show. Most of the slides are shot by an amateur.

Whenever possible, the department tries to use the foster home as a setting for the photographs because children are most comfortable where their toys are readily available. It also helps to be able to call on the foster mother to encourage a child's cooperation. A second choice location is a park or playground.

A telephoto zoom lens is used to take close-up pictures without standing too close to the children. This is particularly good for shy or nervous children and for candid shots. The narrative gives information about the children's personalities, hobbies, pets, and friends.

Films

A documentary film, "One of the Family," is used with prospective adoptive parents and other audiences. In it, foster children tell how they feel about their status and about adoption, and an adoptive placement of an older child is reenacted by the actual adoptive family involved. Three films, which expand upon topics covered in "One of the Family," are also available.

Personal Contact

No publicity program can produce results without a great deal of community involvement and visibility on the part of the agency's administrators and staff. Personal contact is especially essential for recruitment from minority communities. The department's south central office has made great strides in reaching out to the predominantly black community it serves.

Social workers and specially trained adoptive parents often appear as speakers before community groups and in schools and colleges. They usually take a film or a slide show, brochures, and photographs as visual aids.

Index

Index

Abortion: and changes in adoption agencies' policies, 9–11; and decline in relinquishment of babies, 9–10, 22, 99, 100; effect of on adoption statistics, 2

Acceptance rates of adoption agencies, 3–6, 57–60

Adoption agencies: acceptance rates of, 3–6, 57–60; and adoption failures, 77–80, 84–86; adoption trends (1964-1974), 99, 100; black-adoption oriented, 17, 21–23, 27, 43–60, 122–129; black adoption, percentages of, 22, 29, 51, 56, 58; counseling services of, for black mothers, 6–9; effectiveness of adoption exchange services, 14–15; and effectiveness of black social workers, 32, 35–38, 71; effects of legal abortions on, 9–11; failure rates of, 77–86; funding of, 15, 22, 29, 33–34, 122–123; and impact of social work profession on black adoptions, 80–86; independent adoptions as alternative to, 15–16; informal referral, system of, 24–26; and international adoptions, 15; methods of, for reducing oversupply of black babies, 9; and obstacles to adoption of foster children, 11–14; outreach programs of, 27–28, 29; and outside pressure for more black adoptions, 21–23; policies and attitudes of, on black adoptions, 21, 23–24, 25; policies of private, 5; size of, and involvement with black adopters, 32–33; statistical analysis of increased black adoptions, 35–38; and sympathetic processing for black clients, 28–32; territory served by, and number of black adoptions, 34–35; and transracial adoptions, 94–100. *See also* Black adoptions; Black adoptive families; Black social agencies, for adoption; Public adoption agencies; Social workers; Transracial adoptions; White adoptive families

Adoption exchanges, 14–15

Adoption failures: rate of, 78; social worker's fear of, 84–85; as unavoidable, 79–80

Adoption fees: of black adoption agencies, 31, 126; and discouragement of black adopters, 9, 31

Adoption process: at Homes for Black Children, 124–126; at New York City Division of Adoptive Services, 48–53; and sympathetic processing, 28–32

Adoption Resource Exchange of North America, 16

Adoptive parent organizations, 93–94, 99

Adoptive parents. *See* Black adoptive families; White adoptive families

Age: of applicants approved by New York City Division of Adoptive Services, 45–48; effect of mother's, on acceptance by adoption agencies, 3–5; significance of, in adoption of children, 16, 79

Altstein, Howard, 100, 101, 102, 108, 109, 110

American Civil Liberties Union, 92

American Indian children, adoption of, by white parents, 93, 97

Antimiscegenation laws, 89–90

Appointments, social worker's influence on clients keeping, 30, 67–68

Baltimore, City Department of Social Services, black adoption program of, 17

Baltimore, Maryland, study of adoption agencies in, 21–39

Bernstein, Rose, 9, 83

Billingsley, Andrew, 9, 26

149

About the Author

Dawn Day is an associate project director at Response Analysis Corporation in Princeton, New Jersey. She holds a bachelor's degree in economics from Oberlin College, and a master's degree in social work and a Ph.D. in sociology from the University of Michigan. She has had a continuing concern with racial discrimination in the United States. She is author of *The Negro and Discrimination in Employment* and coauthor of *Protest, Politics and Prosperity* and the *American Energy Consumer.*